CW00860443

Acknowledgements

I could not have written this book without the years of support from my kinky friends and family. I would especially like to thank innocent secrets for her tireless work proofreading, editing, and creating artwork for this book, as well as Mistress Gemini, DarkNicht for their support and valuable suggestions, and Pandora for her tips regarding rubber bands, and for her emotional support during difficult transitional periods in my life. In addition, I would like to thank all of those individuals at the Dominion in West LA, who provided a beautifully well kept and safe space where young fledgling Dominas could work, explore, and gain mentorship from other Ladies. I would also like to take this moment to pause in gratitude for the numerous individuals who took time to train me in proper singletail technique, bondage methods, and other protocol. Without the invaluable experience and support from all of these individuals, this book would not have been possible.

Preface

Although there are many amazingly good books about BDSM, I was surprised to have found that there are very few references available for professional Dominatrixes, also known as Pro-Dommes. Although this book is a valuable resource for lifestyle Dominas as well, it is specifically meant for professionals, especially those who may live in remote areas, who might have trouble finding a local dungeon to train with.

This book is an introduction into various BDSM ideas, concepts, and a few business practices important to know for Pro-Dommes who want to create a successful and profitable practice. It does not describe how to do amazing bondage, the proper way to deliver corporal punishment, or how to safely perform tantric fire play. It is less of a "how to" manual as much as it is a way to gain a deeper understanding into the mindset of the submissive male, and a way to learn some common business practices for Pro-Dominas that can only be learned from other Dommes.

Because this book is designed for Pro-Dommes, I have taken the customary practice used within the FemDom community of capitalizing the words, Dominatrix, Domina, Domme, and Lady, as well as Queen, and using the lower case for the submissive males. Because this is a book for professionals, the words submissive, sub, bottom, and client have been used interchangeably to denote the person paying for the service. It is understood that clients come from varying backgrounds of all races and nationalities, and can also be transgendered, queer, female, or even a couple, but because 99% of those who pay for professional Dominatrix services are men, the male pronouns have been used to denote the submissive, bottom and client.

It is my wish to provide a comprehensive introduction to Professional Dominatrix work to those who are considering working professionally but have not yet undergone the extensive training and gained the experience required in order to perform their duties well. This book will provide an introduction in clear, concise language and is a reference only, and is not meant to be a substitute for proper mentorship and hands on training. The process of acting in the capacity of a Dominatrix is truly an art form that requires years of training, talent, and skill, and creativity, and is truly the highest order of professional sex work. It is my intention to provide food for thought and resources for the ingenues first starting out which guide them in the right direction.

Table of Contents

۾

Learning the Ropes

Is this for You?

Becoming a Dominatrix, either for profit or for pleasure, is much different than becoming an escort. Granted, there are some very talented and smart escorts, and of course, both Dominatrices and Escorts fall under the umbrella of "sex workers," that is, individuals who cater to the passions, lusts, and sexual desires of their clients (whether or not there is actual sex that takes place,) and as such, are vulnerable to the same sorts of problems that an escort might encounter in her work. Unlike an escort, however, a Dominatrix needs to have very specialized training and knowledge, in addition to people skills, in order to become a Maestra of Craft.

The process of becoming a Maestra of Craft will take place over years, however, you can learn some basics in a matter of months. The types of skills you will need to learn are difficult to pick up solely through reading, or even by watching video instructional. It is essential to have hands on training, and also to have a community support network who can share their experiences and help you through difficulties that you may encounter not only through your work and play, but through the personal repercussions that you may experience with your vanilla friends and family who may not be quite accepting of your lifestyle choices.

While placing an ad on one of the various advertising sites used by Pro-Dommes will allow you to immediately begin taking calls, that does not mean that you will be properly trained for BDSM activities, or psychologically prepared for the types of situations you will experience. It is very important to begin the process slowly, do some initial reading, and take the proper hands on training before taking the plunge. While I do not address the psychological issues, specific stresses, and moral dilemmas that some Ladies may face during the course of their job, I do provide important training information, and address the most important practical and safety considerations important to the Professional Dominatrix.

Local Leather Groups

Finding a local leather organization is a wonderful way to begin your learning process. Most major cities will have an S&M meetup group which will offer lectures and hands on workshops in various skills from basic bondage, to percussive play, to single tail skills. You may have to do a bit of research online if you live in a smaller community, but inevitably, you will be able to find a lecture group, workshop, or party within one to two hours of where you live.

Your Local BDSM Boutique

If you live in a small city, one of your best bets to find parties and community is to head in to your local kinky boutique, and by this I mean a place that sells BDSM supplies and clothing. I'm not talking about stores that carry furry handcuffs and cheap blindfolds, but the ones that carry electro-play gear and single tails. More often than not, this type of store might even offer classes, and at the very least, will probably have a bulletin board with flyers for events and parties. In the old days before the internet, if you were in a new town, this would be how you would find cool events, local BDSM clubs, and newspapers with ProDomme advertising.

Workshops

There are lots of workshops and even entire Conventions dedicated to the practice of BDSM. You may have to do a road trip or travel a bit to find one, but the contacts and knowledge that you will gain from doing this will be more than worth it! See resources section to find a few recommended.

Working at a Local Dungeon
Working at a local dungeon is by far one of the best ways to network and find mentorship. Many well respected Dommes begin their foray into Dominance by switching. This may or may not be your thing, especially if you are a lifestyle Dominant, but switching can provide an invaluable insight into what a bottom experiences during a BDSM scene. You will learn the difference between pleasurable and intolerably painful sensations, and learn a little about other's topping styles. Also, you will learn quite a lot about technique simply by watching and experiencing, and you may learn things that you might never have learned simply by starting out as a Dominant.

Finding a Mentor
You do not necessarily have to switch in order to be a top rate Domme, however, you do need to have a mentor. This can be kind of tricky, as a mentor should be someone who has have had enough training and experience themselves in order to be able to teach another person. The best way to find a mentor is to go to play parties and watch and network with others. You should find a mentor who inspires you and who is a Mistress (or Master) of craft themselves so that you might learn from the best. Of course, you will have to have the right rapport with them in order that they will be willing to take the time and effort to train you. A mentor should be a good friend who you enjoy spending time with aside from the teaching aspect of your training, and of course, you should offer your time and help in some way in order to show your appreciation. Offer to help them clean and condition their leather or other equipment, or help

pack their car for a play party. Let them know that you appreciate their time and the benefit of their experience.

Resources

Social Networking and News
http://collarspace.com - find a lifestyle submissive or bottom
http://fetlife.com - friends, local meet ups, events/parties, and discussion forums
http://okcupid.com - best dating site to find kinksters
https://www.TheLeatherJournal.com - BDSM Newspaper
http://www.GreatLakesDen.net - Midwest Region Newspaper

Conventions
http://www.ArizonaFetishSociety.com - Arizona Fetish
Events   http://www.BeatMeinStlL.com - St Louis, Missouri
http://www.BondCon.com - Bondage Convention - location varies
http://DarkOdyssey.com - East Coast Camping, Community, Play Party, Lectures
http://www.DomCon.com - Pro Domme Convention New Orleans and other
locations http://www.DomConLA.com - ProDomme Convention Los Angeles
http://www.FetishCon.com - St Petersburg, Florida
http://TheFloatingWorld.org - Kinky Vacations, Community, Workshops
http://www.FolsomStreetEvents.org - BDSM street fair, San Fransisco and
New York http://www.kinkfest.org - Portland OR
http://www.LasVegasSmokeout.com - Las Vegas, NV
http://www.LeatherWeekend.com - Washington DC
http://www.imslfoundation.org - International MS Leather, Bay Area, CA http://
www.ShibariCon.com - Chicago
http://www.SouthPlainsLeatherfest.com - Dallas, Texas
 http://www.SouthwestLeather.org - Arizona

Leather Pride Events
http://www.AtlantaEagle.com - Atlanta, Georgia
https://www.facebook.com/LeatherPrideBelgium- Belgium
(Europe) also http://www.leatherpride.be
https://www.facebook.com/DCLeatherPride - Washington
DC   http://www.DesertLeatherPride.com - Palm
Springs, California https://LosAngelesLeatherPride.com -

Los Angeles, California
http://www.MNLeatherPride.org - Minnesota
http://www.PortlandLeather.org/home.php - Portland,
Oregon http://plpn.org/history- Philadelphia, Pennslyvania
http://www.SDLeatherPride.com - San Diego, California
 http://SFLeather.org - San Fransisco, CA
http://TorontoLeatherPride.ca - Toronto, Canada_____
http://www.TheEagleAmsterdam.com - Amsterdam
(Europe) http://UKLeatherPride.com - Bristol, Manchester,
UK   http://www.wsmlo.org - Washington

Dungeon/ProDomme Finders
http://Backpage.com - list style advertising
http://CityVibe.com - erotic advertising_____
http://DickieVirgin.com -ads and link
exchanges
http://ErosGuide.com - higher end erotic
advertising http://MistressReview.net -
ProDomme listings
http://OpenAdultDirectory/BDSM - dungeon and ProDomme directory
http://Pandemos.net - Dungeon and ProDomme listings

Written Material

Screw the Roses, Send Me the Thorns: The Romance and Sexual
Sorcery of Sadomasochism, C 1995, by Phillip Miller and Molly Devon

Jay Wiseman's Erotic Bondage Handbook, c 2000, by Jay Wiseman

The Seductive Art of Japanese Bondage, c 2002, by Midori and Craig
Morey

The Mistress Manual c 200 by Mistress Lorilei

Venus in Furs, by Leopold Von Sacher-Masoch

Various Writings of Marquis de Sade

Domme Personae

What is your Dominatrix Persona? Are you aloof and unattainable? The impossible, Demanding Diva? Or deeply maternal, yet stern and demanding? Like the bottoming personae of your clients, you will find that you will be more or less one of these types (or perhaps a blend of two.)

The Seductress
Beautiful, alluring, possessed of many charms, and slightly mysterious, you are the femme fatale! Like Helen of Troy and Cleopatra, powerful men will lay down their arms (or take them up) in order to please you. Whether bohemian or well heeled, you have a trademark style that exudes sexuality, and at times can be flashy and ostentatious. Whether or not you are soft spoken, you are more likely to use your charms and powers of suggestion to achieve your aims rather than brute force, and you can be exceptionally devious, psychologically manipulative, and conniving when your jealousies and suspicions are aroused. You love being taken out on the town, dancing, and anywhere where there is a glamorous party and excitement.

The Boss
Intelligent, worldly, and well spoken, you have a strong sense of integrity and command respect without needing to raise your voice or use force. You have a direct way of speaking that immediately gets other's attention. You don't need to dress like a harlot in order to display your sex appeal; it comes from simply being confidently in charge. As a business professional, you would wear a well tailored skirt and conservative blouse with heels, but as a Domme you might wear a black full length catsuit that displays your curves without showing too much

skin and sturdy boots. Your punishments are meted out fairly, in a calm and rational manner, but you are ultimately unattainable and aloof to all men except the ultimately alpha. Nurses and Doctor Dominants fall into this category as well.

The Queen or Royal Lady
Always impeccably well dressed, you have myriad servants to do your bidding, and spend your time with the concerns of your empire, and of course, pampering treatments. Refined and well read, you have eclectic knowledge of arts, literature, cuisine, and of course, the art of punishment and keeping of slaves. Although commanding and Dominant, at times you can be tyrannical and fly into rages. You crave adoration above all else and love to have men grovel at your well heeled feet, worshiping them. You also demand expensive shopping trips from your suitors and like to eat at Zagat rated restaurants.

The Warrior Princess
Strong and independent, you don't need men to do your bidding, however, your passion and untamed beauty causes men to fall fast and hard for you. Your technical knowledge of bondage and the art of warfare is unmatched, and you are equally as likely to be seen taking your crossbow or rifle out for target practice as you are to be seen at a public event with your fellow knights. You are known to quickly and skillfully physically submit any man who dares challenge you, yet you have a rugged style both in clothing and in manner and a selflessness that will inspire your subservients to emulate you by enduring incredible trials for you. As a Domina, you might be a Military Maiden, Police Woman, or Gladiatrix.

The Goddess

Free spirited and earthy, you are likely to be well versed in the arts of tantra, yoga, and natural health. Your play space is scented with incense and home made candles, and although you are stern and demanding, you are also deeply maternal. You are likely to be crafty and have numerous home made toys and tools of the trade. You have a wide range of emotions and the thunder of your anger can quickly recede into the soft gentle sunlight of your gentle nurturing and appreciation. Men are drawn to you in a very organic, visceral, powerful way.

The Dominatrixes that I have known over the years are as individual as the leaves on a tree - no two are alike. Although it is okay to channel an idol, literary character, or notorious villainess for intense role play scenes, ultimately, your best tactic is to be genuine to your true impulses, and to do what you enjoy doing.

Dressing for Success

The importance of the right outfit should not be underestimated for a Dominatrix, especially in the case of a fetish session, and even masochists prefer to session with a beautifully dressed woman. Here are some common clothing requests.

Leather - Yes, the 80s have long since passed, but in the S&M scene, leather is still a very common request. Leather (as well as leatherette and PVC) mini skirts are easy to come by, and essential for any Dominatrix wardrobe. My leather and PVC mini skirts are my most common wardrobe request, followed by my knee high stiletto boots.

Full Length Catsuits - surprisingly enough, sometimes the less skin you show, the better, especially if you are clad in skin tight PVC or latex. This is a very common fetish, and I once had a TV producer client tell me that the reason that he called me was that he saw a photo of me in one of my advertisements in which I was entirely covered in PVC. Cyberskin clothing is very popular with fetishists,

Latex Clothing - skirts and fantasy clothing. At the minimum, you should have at least one latex dress that zips. Latex clothing is exceptionally difficult to put on without zippers, and needs to be powdered or put on using dressing aid, and then it needs to be shined. Truly, wearing latex clothing is a labor of love. Latex stockings are fairly easy to find online and are also a nice addition to a fetish wardrobe.

Before putting on latex clothing, make sure your nails are trimmed and filed, and you have removed any sharp jewelry. If you are using dressing aid, apply to the area of your body that you will be dressing first, and then carefully (and very *slowly*) slide on the latex. Even though it is stretchy, treat your latex like the most delicate of silk stockings. Carefully gather it up in the same way you would a stocking, and let out the gathered parts a little at a time as you slide into the garment. If you are using powder, powder the inside of the garment liberally before sliding it on. Do *not* wear body lotion or oil because it will eat away the latex. A specially made latex shine should be used after dressing to shine your garment. As a last resort, you can use water, but you will get a spotty finish.

Corsets - These happen to be my personal favorite, and they offer instant waist slimming and can be worn over a cute black mini dress paired with high heels from any department store for an instant fetish look. A quality, steel boned lace up corset is a wonderful addition to any fetish wardrobe. There are many corset impersonators out there, including bustiers with lacing and body slimmers. Pay a bit extra and get the steel boned version in the proper size. It will last much longer and make you look like a million dollars.

Boots - As in the David Bowie song "Venus in Furs", the iconic black stiletto boot is the most important footwear that you will own, will be big money makers if you will be doing boot worship sessions. These are one of my top wardrobe requests, and I recommend getting a good quality pair that fits well, since you will be standing for long hours in them. I once bought a nice pair that needs to be laced up each time it is worn, which takes a lot of time, and the hardware on the front prevented me from being able to kneel down while I was tying some knots in some rope on a sub. Although they looked good in the photos and were very highly requested for sessions, I recommend having at least one pair of boots that can be quickly zipped up and ready to go in a minute or two. Fetish clothing takes a long time to put on, so keep that in mind while you are shopping.

Peep Toe Heels or High Heeled Sandals - Common request for foot fetishists, and for the   most part are easy to find at department stores and shoe boutiques.

Classic Stiletto Pumps - You will need these for office style role play.

Stockings - both cuban foot stockings and standard, waist length nude stockings are common requests, and they look gorgeous. To properly put on cuban foot stockings, gather up the stocking carefully. Standing with your back to a mirror, place your index finger and thumb on the seam of the stocking, and move your index and thumb to the place where you want the seam to be as you are sliding up the stocking. Seams are hard to adjust after stockings are put on, and I am lucky that my Goth Goddess friend taught me this secret as we were getting ready for a fetish ball years ago.

Opera or elbow length gloves - These are important to have, and should be in latex or cyber   skin of some kind. I personally prefer the fingerless kind, since it is virtually impossible to answer your smart phone or use a trackpad on your computer while your fingertips are clad in latex.

Makeup- Remember that as a Dominatrix you are selling a very particular fantasy, and that is of an exotic, otherworldly, unattainable Goddess. Exaggerated eyes, lips and fantasy makeup is ideal. I know lots of Dominas who go through the effort of putting on false eyelashes, theatrical contact lenses, and have even had their nails filed into spikes or had fangs permanently affixed to their teeth. You don't have to go to some of these extremes, but make sure you look fabulous.

Although I have listed off some commonly requested clothing, ultimately, your wardrobe must reflect your style, personality, and sensibilities. Your accessories and makeup should be an outward expression of your innermost impulses and a Dominant Lady. Fetish clothing can be very pricey, and you will necessarily need to start with one or two nice pieces, and gather more slowly as you continue working. Remember, shopping trips are one of the most exciting things for submissive men! Inevitably, you will be given gifts and small tokens of affection whether you ask for them or not.

Creating the Magic

As the Domme, *YOU* will be in charge of everything, not only the activities for the scene, but the mood and tempo of the session. Anyone who is familiar with Carlos Castenenda's work knows that creating magic partly involves changing your perception about reality, and as your perception changes, you will also change the perception in your subs. You are part Goddess, part bodyworker, and part alchemist who has knowledge of dark arts that others yearn to explore. Remember that you are creating the *fantasy version*   of the kidnapping, interrogation, domestic discipline situation, or other scenario. Keep in mind that the situation is mutually pleasurable for both Domme and sub, and that you are a trained professional who is providing a service (albeit as Goddess who is worshipped and often asked to do whatever she wishes.) What you might do with your own personal subs might be very different from what you might do with a brand new client who you have never seen before. There are times to push limits, with those who you have established a deep rapport and have had an ongoing relationship with, and there are times when you should use your best judgement and hold back, even if your bottom begs and implores you to offer more abuse.

Establishing Trust and the Negotiation

BDSM scenesters refer to the discussion of likes and dislikes and what will occur in the session as a "negotiation." The negotiation might take place on the phone or through email, but often it occurs in person, at a diner or local coffee place. During the negotiation, you should find out about your bottom's previous experience, the types of activities they like and dislike, and what he might like to try. Discuss any specific fantasy scenarios including wardrobe for both Top and bottom, as well as any important health concerns, surgeries, and other major medical problems that might pose safety issues for the bottom during your session. You should clarify if there are any "safewords" that your bottom prefers to use to indicate that they want to stop activity. Answer any questions that they might have regarding safety issues. Doing this is important for informational purposes, but it is also a very good way to establish trust with your bottom. He will know that even though he might be in a precarious, frightening, or painful situation, that he will trust your level of competence and know that he will "have an out" if necessary.

Lighting

Even a bare room can change into a wonderland with the right type of lighting. Candles, colorful LED lights, and even projection machines are relatively inexpensive, and are a very important part of your dungeon or play room ambience. What type of mood are you trying to create? Dark and forboding? Soft and sensual? Racy and provocative? Changing the mood in your room can be as simple as throwing a colored scarf over the lamp shade and wrapping it around the stand (a method I use often for hotel rooms which is fast and simple) and candles create a sense of romance and mystery. Generally, lower lighting conditions are preferable for BDSM scenes, but surprisingly, quite a few people like to play in bright lighting. It really depends upon your scene and your preference.

Music

Perhaps more than any other element, the right music can be essential to creating the right type of mood. Choose lighter or lounge style music for a more sensual session, or darker, more somber, or music with a driving beat for an intense physical or psychological session. Although you may enjoy punk rock, goth, hard rock, or edgy electronic music, consider the fact that many of your bottoms will be relatively conservative, middle aged professionals. Although ultimately your music must reflect and appeal to YOU, plan your session as if you were planning a party and consider the tastes and needs of your guest.

Scent

Our sense of smell plays a very powerful role in the perceptions of our psyche. Scents can bring back memories from years past, relax and calm, or invigorate and arouse. Scented candles and incense can be used to cleanse the air in your space, and also to create a particular mood. Looking to create a sense of suspense? Try heavier, muskier scents or even industrial ones. Looking to create a sensual ambience? Use heavy florals and aphrodisiacs. Make sure you have taken out your garbage, and if necessary, have aired out the room after a previous session has left. Nothing can kill the mood more than walking into a room that reeks of another sub's sweat from two hours ago.

Appearance and Furnishings

If you are sessioning from home, make sure that your play space is neat and orderly, and that walkways are clear from objects and debris. Remember that you will have a bound, perhaps blindfolded and gagged submissive wandering through your space. Even if you are guiding them, older bottoms and those with physical disabilities may find it harder to get around. You will be ultimately responsible for everything that happens in your session, so make sure your space is free from falling objects, breakables, and safety hazards that might be dangerous. You will need to notify blindfolded bottoms of steps and other things in their path as you lead them. You should have furniture in your space that is play friendly, such as armless chairs for OTK spankings, and strong and sturdy chairs with lots of anchor points for bondage at the minimum. Very well equipped spaces might have a spanking horse or bench, bondage beds, a Saint Andrew's Cross or stockade, or other dungeon furniture, and perhaps a cage or jail cell. Don't forget to have a dense foam pillow or meditation pillow for your subs to kneel on. Unless you have wall to wall carpet, this is a practical and useful item to have as part of your kinky inventory, and it allows your bottoms to kneel for much longer times for your pleasure. You can also use this pillow to support the hips and chests of your subs while they are in bondage on the floor. If you prefer, instead of a pillow you can opt to find good quality knee pads that you can make your sub wear while they crawl for you.

The Build-up

Take your cue from the Burlesque greats of the last century, like Bettie Page and Tempest Storm. Build up the intensity of the scene slowly, and gauge your bottom's response carefully by their body language and their verbal feedback. Are they arching towards you and licking their lips? Or are they trying to shield themselves? Are they emitting high pitched screams? Or are they groaning softly in ecstasy? The response that you want will depend greatly upon the bottom, whether they are a masochist, and their level of experience. Sometimes, high pitched screams might be what you are going for. Don't do all the activities that your sub requested in the negotiation, and before engaging in very intense activities such as caning, test a new bottom with a few light strokes to see how they respond. Just like a good burlesque dancer, you will want to tease, tease, tease, and *deny* ultimate satisfaction. Leave something to look forward to for the next session. This does not mean you can't let your sub finish themselves off, or that you can't follow a scripted scenario on occasion. It means that you are in charge of the session and that part of the fun for your sub is the unpredictability of knowing that you have ultimate control. Keep things fresh in small ways, not only for your sub, but for your own satisfaction.

Submissive Psychology

The most important thing for new Dommes to understand is that while you can get anyone to submit to you, not everyone is "submissive." In fact, there are various categories of bottoms who are not very submissive at all! Some of the most common types that you will encounter are listed below.

Bottoms

The term bottom simply connotes the person who is being Dominated, and thus bottoms need not be classically submissive. Generally, they get turned on by having someone else be temporarily in control for a short time, and can also be be masochists or fetishists, but they can be very demanding and difficult to work with. This might be the guy who wants you to wrestle him into submission, forcibly kidnap him, or hypnotize him into cooperation. I usually think of a "bottom" as a non submissive masochist who gets off on female aggression, if a straight male, or a non submissive masochist who is a thrill seeker, male or female.

Fetishists

Fetishist are not slaves, and may or may not be submissive and/or into pain. Generally, a fetishist may call you for a particular activity or clothing item, and they can be extremely particular. For instance, a latex fetishist may want to see you in a particular pair of latex pants, and if the pants deviate too much from his idea of the ideal, he may not want to do the session. He may get turned on by watching you crush grapes with your pedicured feet, or polishing your latex while you are wearing it, or putting on silk Cuban foot stockings. Some fetishists have a submissive streak, but not all.

Masochists

Masochists love pain, usually of a specific type, as in nipple torture or CBT, maybe electro-play, needles, cutting, and of course, corporal punishment! They will instruct you as to exactly how they want to be tortured and correct you if you're not doing it to their satisfaction. Masochists are known to bring their own tools and equipment and will give you lots of feedback when the like the stimulation that you are doling out. They are not shy about asking for what they want, and can be known to "top from the bottom."

Submissives

Submissive enjoy giving up control to a beautiful, powerful, demanding woman who excites them. They might be into verbal humiliation, hypnosis, power tripping on the part of the Domme, non physical forms of control with the exception of light bondage collar and lead. Most true submissives will submit to a certain amount of light to moderate pain and discomfort in order to please their Domme, although they don't love pain the way that a masochist does. What they do love is being vulnerable and giving up control to an authority/power figure.

My personal favorite subcategory of submissives is the person I like to call the "alpha sub." Alpha sub has a very prestigious, demanding job and a public face. He loves to give over control and loves being toyed with, but does not like to be degraded. He can be coerced into deep submission, but lets it be known that he is there of his own free will and can leave at any time. Other submissives can be easily coerced into doing things that they really don't want to do, and may become resentful after the fact. They will not say anything about their reservations during the session with you, but may write a negative review or gossip with other Dommes or scenesters about your thoughtlessness or unwarranted cruelty. When dealing with an extreme submissive, it is advisable to have a pre-session negotiation checklist filled out and signed. This is an easier way of getting the often shy submissive to open up about their fantasies, and that way you can also cover your own behind by showing them their requests after the session if they complain.

Submissive Masochists
These are the stuff of Dominant wet dreams! They will submit to extreme pain, go through unthinkable trials and perform superhuman feats for you. They are the ones who tell you that they do not need a safe word, but keep in mind, you should take extra care with this type of playmate, because they will often push themselves to go further than they should, which can result in terrible psychological/medical sequelae. I always suggest taking it slow when playing with a new person, and building up slowly. After all, if you take it from zero to sixty in two seconds, what will your play partner have to look forward to in future sessions?

The PET
Like a spoiled, doted over family pet, the pet craves attention at all times, loves to be adorned with body jewelry and new outfits, and loves to be shown off at parties. Usually females or younger males, pets are prince/sses who want the fantasy of being with a powerful Domme, but like to be pampered, wined and dined, and taken shopping to be able to wear things that please the Domme. They will often submit to all sorts of things to be with the Domme, and in general they like being overpowered. Pets will charm you with their beauty, coquettishness, and doleful manner, but tread carefully! Pets have well developed egos peppered with various insecurities, and small affronts can set them off. I've had a cute boy or two that can fall into this category.

The Pig

The flip side of the pet is the pig. If you have a creative streak and love to talk nasty, you will have lots of fun with the pig. They enjoy verbal abuse, all types of humiliation, being spat on, used as furniture in public places, used as ashtrays, and will usually thank you profusely for all sorts of punishment doled out to them. The pig is almost always submissive as well, but might also be a very alpha type who simply enjoys the psychological thrill of being humiliated. They may get very submissive while under your charge, and suddenly turn into a different person when the session is over.

Curious Romantics

These are artists, photographers, academics, high level business types who like like the intellectual thrill of trying new things and the erotic charge of letting a Dominant woman take control. They're not sure what they like, but they like the fantasy of a beautiful woman wearing fetish attire putting them in compromising situations. They usually tend to be experimental enough to submit to light punishment and maybe light forms of pain, and they enjoy role play and lots of provocative talk and verbal interaction. It may even be a good idea to give them a tour of your dungeon or home play space and explain how certain equipment is used, and perhaps discuss into session protocol and use of safe words so that there are no surprises. This will put them at ease and make the whole session run more smoothly.

The Doormat

A category that you want to avoid at all costs, doormats are those who just can't get any sort of sexual attention at all without either paying for it or making themselves a doormat. Both men and women fall into this category. They usually have poor self esteem and may vacillate between loving the attention and loathing themselves for acting so low, and may eventually take out their suppressed rage against you in various sorts of passive aggressive ways. Although it's okay to see doormats for professional sessions, you definitely don't want to have them as personal slaves.

***

With experience, you will be able to conduct a short interview, often called a "negotiation," with a client and quickly determine what categories they fall into. Generally, a particular client will fall into two or three categories. You will quickly learn what motivates them, and how you can push their buttons in order to achieve the desired effect of maximum submission to plunge them deep into subspace!

Session Types

BDSM

Ladies who are new to the practice of BDSM and fetishism are often a little shocked, and oftentimes have a hard time understanding the motives and desires of their submissive clients. This section is designed to give you a very brief synopsis of what types of requests you may get as a Pro-Domme.

Adult Baby
These session requests are rare, but the basic idea is that you will treat the sub just like a baby, feeding him baby food, clothing him, changing diapers, powdering, etc. I get these requests so rarely that I don't keep supplies for this, and generally adult babies will offer to bring their own diapers, clothing, and supplies. These sessions are all about the sub getting attention from you, so in that sense you will be something of a "service top" which means a top who is going through the motions to please the sub, and this is why some Dommes will not accept these types of sessions. They tend to be fairly easy, but if you do not wish to change soiled diapers, you should notify the sub before the session. Men who call for adult baby sessions are primarily seeking nurturing, the warm feeling that they get from being cared for and doted over, mixed with the mild humiliation that they feel from being emasculated in this way.

Ball Busting
This session involves kicking and crushing a man's scrotum and testes with your feet and heels. Don't forget that it is pleasurable, if not always the pain, then the act of submitting to this type of abuse. Oftentimes that

victim will have a raging erection while being ball busted. There are some safety techniques and proper methods that a good mentor can teach you, however, this is one of the few sessions which inevitably will involve lots of pain and some minor to major injury, regardless of how it is done. The act of submitting to this can be so arousing for the recipient that I have had at least one occasion of a man ejaculating simply from having me step on his scrotum.

Caught with His Pants Down

In this scenario you have caught your victim in a compromising situation. Perhaps he was masturbating at work, or maybe he was caught having indiscreet sex. The offense need not be sexual, but could be something like money laundering, falsifying documents, or other crime. In any case, this session is less about pain and more about *humiliation* . Spend a lot of time chastising the individual and going through various scenarios in which he might be punished. Threaten to reveal his indiscretions to friends, family, his wife, police, or other individuals who might be shocked or displeased. You might humiliate him by placing him in a cock cage or chastity device, or use some other method for stopping the offending action (for instance, blindfolding him if he was looking at porn, handcuffing him for stealing something.) Finally, you may eventually choose some sort of minor punishment, such as using a ruler to slap his hands in an old world "schoolmaster" style punishment, spanking with a hairbrush as in a domestic style discipline, or using a belt. A more intense punishment might involve spending time in "jail" or submitting to heavy corporal punishment such as caning or a whipping with a singletail.

CBT (Cock and Ball Torture)

This involves genital bondage and various contraptions which crush, weigh down, and torture the penis and scrotum/testes. This is a masochistic session, and the recipient is one who loves pain inflicted by the right Domina. You will need equipment for this session such as crushing vices, parachutes, weights, electro cages, and more.

Corporal/Judicial Punishment

This is the stereotypical Dominatrix activity which is often portrayed in films, generally out of context, and with shocking amounts of violence. Granted, S&M scenes can be extremely intense, but hopefully, you will not want to try to reproduce the last film you have seen. Judicial punishment, as well as other types of punishment, are doled out for a specific offense. A real life example would be an American teenager who is sentenced to public caning across the back after littering in a South Asian country. Believe it or not, these types of punishments are actually considered *minor* sentences in most countries where they are practiced, and are intended to deter the individual from committing further infringements while allowing them to go about their lives without serving jail or prison time. Although this type of session is considered masochistic, the buildup and sexual tension happens during the "sentencing." As is true for this and other types of sessions, the majority of the arousal comes from the nakedness, vulnerability, and humiliation of being punished publicly (or in the privacy of a play space in front of a beautiful, fully clothed Domina. You should put as much time and effort into the sentencing that builds up to the punishment as you do with the punishment itself. Needless to say, as a corporal punishment professional it is imperative that you use proper techniques in order to prevent undue injury so that the punished one can go about his normal business after he leaves your presence.

Cutting, Scarification, Branding, and Play Piercing

Don't do this without a significant amount of education and training! These things can be potentially dangerous unless the proper precautions are taken. Cutting and scarification is a type of body modification that leaves a permanent marking, much like a tattoo. Branding also leaves a permanent mark, and can be a sign of ownership by a Domme over a sub. Play piercing can be temporary or permanent, if a piece of jewelry is inserted. All of these things are equally about the significance of ownership that a ring or mark means on the body of the sub as it is about the pain that must be endured in order to achieve the final product. For most subs, the idea of enduring painful trials for their Domme in order to please them is pleasurable. They also love to proudly show off their signs of ownership to the world.

Domestic and Personal Service

You will get requests from subs who want to clean for you, cook for you, pick up toilet paper or tampons or groceries for you. In this case, the reward for the sub comes from the pleasure that you get by having these things done for you. Some of the subs who ask to clean nude may be exhibitionists. Unless you know that the particular sub enjoys being humiliated, be gracious. If you are especially pleased with their service and want to give them an extra reward, allow them to massage your feet, legs, or back, or to finish themselves off while they kiss your feet. Simply allowing the sub to have contact with your Goddess Form is reward enough for most subs.

Erotic Hypnosis

Surprisingly, this is a fairly common request from submissive men. Erotic Hypnosis is different from obedience training in that it is less physically interactive, and plays upon the submissive male's fantasy of being seduced, controlled, and having his willpower over-ridden by a seductively beautiful Femme Fatale. You will need to have some scripts pre-written, and may want to use pendulums, relaxation music, or other props for your session. Often, you will be dressed in some sort of office or sexy professional attire such as closed toe stilettos and pencil skirts. Erotic hypnosis is hyper sexual and addresses deep seated sexual fantasies and impulses. It usually plays upon some sort of manipulation, as in hypnosis that makes the sub submit to every whim of the Domme, or makes a sub male get in touch with his inner femininity so that he can be forcibly feminized by the Domme.

Fire Play, Wand, and Cupping
You will need training and mentorship for this, but it is very sensual as well as edge play for those with fear of the flames. In addition to special training, you will need special equipment, an understanding of fire safety, an ABC fire extinguisher or fireproof blanket, and burn ointment ready in the event of a need for aftercare.

Financial Domination and Consensual Blackmail
One day a sub emails you, and tells you that he wants to send you gifts and tribute for no reason. He may even offer you photos and personal information such as his address so that you can use it to "blackmail" him. Sounds easy, right? Not necessarily. Financial Domination, or FinDom for short, as well as consensual blackmail are types of play that require a deep psychological understanding of what triggers your sub, or pushes his buttons. He becomes aroused by having a woman make outrageous demands for expensive clothing, dinners, or vacations. He may send you large amounts of money for these things sight unseen in exchange for photos of you and your girlfriends (or even boyfriend) taunting him and

exploiting the fact that you have been benefitting from his generosity. The manipulation must be done in a specific way that arouses and triggers the submissive male, and is different for each sub. Some prefer that you be Queenlike in your demands, while others prefer the Seductress method of sweet talking and manipulation. In any case, experience is key for these types of sessions.

Forced Intoxication

The general idea here is that the victim is forced to ingest or inhale some substance or object. I have done forced intox with cigarette smoke into a specialized mask with a breathing tube in it, as well as fake "chloroforming" with something called "poppers" which you can find at many adult stores. You can also do forced intox with wine and liquor, but with GREAT CAUTION. Alcohol is most likely one of the most dangerous substances you can use for forced intox, and it should not be used if the subject will be driving right after the session. Other substances should be used with great caution and not without a great deal of research and experience. I do not condone the use of illegal substances in sessions, although I know that this often takes place.

Kidnapped or Taken Prisoner

This is one of the more extreme types of sessions that you might do. Unlike other sessions, in which the build-up is extremely important, in this session from the moment the victim walks in the door, they should be immediately taken into custody, handcuffed, and rendered helpless. there may or may not be pain involved, but there will be very intense bondage, movement restrictions, behavior restrictions, and psychological domination such as interrogation and brainwashing. This type of scene requires a good deal of equipment, at the minimum rope, blindfolds, a good quality gag, and handcuffs but you might also want to have hoods, spreader bars, a St Andrew's cross, jail cell, or other bondage furniture, an interrogation light, and other fear inducing equipment, like a bullwhip. The sexual tension in this session is induced by *fear*   , *vulnerability*, and also a bit of *physical dominance* from being roughed up.

Medical Exams

This session, like others, is heavily draws from an overall climate of vulnerability and humiliation. The Domina comes in, fully clothed, while the patient is on the table in a medical gown, underwear, or perhaps nothing at all. She begins asking probing and embarrassing questions and the patient is humiliated... *and aroused*. The Domina then proceeds to make the patient submit to all sorts of humiliating exams and medical treatments, some of which might be mildly to heavily painful, but the patient enjoys being compromised by a beautiful, sexy woman in a staged and therefore *safe* setting where everything has been negotiated prior to the treatment. You will need a medical outfit, stethoscope, notepad and prepared intake questions for this session. A bit of training into how to do a medical exam might be helpful as well.

Medical Play

Dominas often get requests for various types of medical play. Make sure you are properly trained in the particular activities that you will be engaging in prior to the session. These types of sessions are really for Dommes with advanced training and lots of experience, and who also have access to expensive equipment and hard to find supplies.

Obedience Training, Brainwashing, Mind-Control

This can take various forms, but it is generally a Pavlovian style training using a carrot-stick approach that will mold your submissive's impulses to your will. The basic premise is that the submissive, similarly to a dog, must be trained the proper way to respect you, the proper way to stand, address you, worship you, and anything else that you desire. The idea is use both reward and punishment and complete control to manipulate the submissive's hold on reality, making them more mentally malleable and agreeable to your commands. You may want to put them in sensory deprivation for awhile, before interrogating them and training them by immediately rewarding them for desirable behaviors and immediately punishing them for undesired behavior. You can use shock collars, CorPun equipment, gags, humiliation, food rewards, and threats of blackmail to encourage desired behaviors. Obedience training is more physically interactive than Erotic Hypnosis, but both of these things play upon the submissive male's wish to be manipulated and controlled.

The Abuse Pig

The abuse pig wants to be utterly and totally degraded, often in very disgusting ways. They generally want to be spat upon, face slapped, and spoken to in a very nasty, degrading fashion. They may want to be used as an ashtray or be covered with disgusting objects. The most important skill you will need for this session is your ability to talk trash, pure and simple. The more mean and nasty that you can be, the better. From experience, I have discovered that the sexual tension in this type of session derives not only from the humiliation, but also from the gross out factor from being treated in this way. I have done smothering sessions during which the bottom has begged and pleaded to be farted upon. While it seems inconceivable to most people that this could be a turn on, there is something about "a nasty thing coming from a sweet innocent beautiful woman" that is a complete turn on.

Sensory Deprivation

Sensory deprivation involves use of special hoods which restrict or inhibit hearing and vision, and other special equipment such as tanks or padded body bags which restrict movement. Remember that even if the client requests "abandonment" you should never completely leave the client unattended for safety reasons. It is best that you put them in a position in which they are not able to see or hear you, so that you can check in occasionally unnoticed. Make sure you take a full medical history and address any unique health and safety concerns of the sub before planning long sessions in which they will be unattended at times.

The Sensual Session

Although a phone call from someone asking for a "sensual session" is sometimes a code for sex, in general a sensual session is more about giving up control, sensory deprivation, and submitting to interesting sensual experiences. A typical session might involve blindfolding the submissive, light bondage, light flogging with suede or fur, vampire gloves, Whartonburg wheels, fire wands, and other equipment which is not necessarily painful but provide interesting sensations. This session is almost more like a type of bodywork, and as anyone who has received a tender and loving flogging knows, it is almost like a percussive massage. As usual, don't neglect the psychological aspect of taking control! Remember, ultimately the client is coming to see *YOU* and your energy, voice, personality and creativity are paramount.

Sissies and Sluts

Sissies are men who need to be feminized, but in a very demure and obedient way. They love to be taught good manners, how to curtsy properly, how to behave like a good girl and a nice lady. Sissies are also sometimes babies who need to be nurtured, mothered, and mildly humiliated. Sluts are the out of control, teenage raging hormone driven version and are overtly sexual. Sluts dress in very provocative clothing and lingerie and love nasty talk and acknowledgement of how dirty and slutty they are. They often need to be made more slutty than they already are. Don't confuse a sissy with a slut simply because they both like to cross dress.

Size Shaming
Size shaming is the act of verbally humiliating a man about his penis size. Most times, the sub who requests this will have a smaller than normal penis size, but sometimes, the sub just becomes aroused from the verbal humiliation, denial of sexual pleasure, and humiliating names for his penis. You may want to refer to his male part as his "teeny peenie" or his "little nub" or even his "worthless flesh." Size shaming can also involve measurements taken at various times that are recorded, both before and after punishment or medical "treatments" that attempt to correct his physical shortcomings. It may also involve taking photos which are used to threaten the sub with blackmail.

Smoke Blowing, Human Ashtray, and Burns
Unlike forced intox, Smoking fetishes are more about the hypnotic effect of the smoke being blown from the lips of the Goddess, and the humiliation of being treated as a receptacle of refuse (whether it be air, ash, or even cigarette butts.) Occasionally, a bottom may even request mild burns. Be prepared to provide aftercare for any session involving burns.

Smothering
This can be done with the hand, but it is most often done by sitting over the bottom' face wearing some type of fetish attire, often PVC or latex

pants (make sure you don't have a zipper in the crotch of the pants because they will leave abrasive cuts and marks on the bottom's face and nose.) The idea is to temporarily cut off the air supply to the bottom, giving them a head rush, both because of the lack of oxygen and also because of the fear and arousal involved with this kind of edge play. Since the bottom with not be able to use their safe word, I generally give them a hand or "safe signal" so that they can signal to stop at any time.

Trampling
The Domme walks over the bottom in bare feet or in some sort of requested footwear, often times heels or boots. There is a safe way to trample and there are certain areas which should never, ever have pressure placed upon them. You will need some training in order to do this properly.

Wrestling and Human Punching Bag
Here, the turn on is female aggression and physicality, and to be overpowered by a strong, Dominant woman. Undoubtedly, the idea of rolling around with a beautiful, strong Superheroine is appealing. It's understood that you will need some training in boxing, and quite a bit of training in wrestling in order to participate in these activities. Wear a sexy bodysuit or shorts and tank top for this session, and on occasion you might be asked to wear a martial arts Gi. This session would definitely qualify as a bit masochistic. As in trampling, there is a safe way to gut punch your sub and a dangerous way of punching their ribcage that should be avoided.

Fetishes

For Dommes who are just starting out, sometimes the hardest sessions for them to come to terms with are the fetish sessions. It is often hard to understand what a guy might find attractive about a pair of dirty gym shoes, for instance, or what might be a turn on about a body odor that most people would find offensive. A fetish is a sexual arousal that comes from a particular object that arouses sexual desire, oftentimes which is not generally associated with sexual arousal. Some of these fetishes may be combined with BDSM sessions. Here are some of the more common ones.

Body Aroma Fetishes

I remember the first time I got a call from someone who wanted to see me for a sweat fetish. He has asked me to come to play on a hot day without showering that morning or the night before. Remember that part of sexual arousal centers around pheromones and our sense of smell. It's my belief that pheromones are the source of arousal surrounding this fetish more than the gross factor. You might decide to "force" your victim to smell your underarms, physically push him around while you are sweaty, demand that he smell different parts of you as he becomes more and more aroused. it is my belief that body odor, like clothing fetishes, are an element of *every single session that I do*, and this is why I don't generally wear deodorant or other products that mask my natural body aroma.

Foot, stocking, boot, and footwear worship

These sessions tend to be quite brief, usually half an hour or less, but be prepared for them to occasionally run longer. I once had a foot and leg worship session that lasted one hour and a half, and involved fruit being eaten from my toes, and honey being massaged into my legs. Most often, the session will involve the client kissing, rubbing, and massaging your feet, licking your boots and smelling them, or having you use him as a footrest while he finishes himself off by hand. Other sessions might involve trampling in bare feet, being kicked or hit with feet, footwear, or boots, or having these things used in aggressive ways. The sexual arousal here is derived primarily by the object of the fetish, whether it be the bare feet, or the footwear, or other item of clothing, such as stockings. Even though the object is at the center of the session, don't forget to engage the client in a suggestive train of conversation regarding the fetish, activity, and how it arouses him, and don't forget about the ritual surrounding most fetishes.

Feminization, Role Reversal, and Cross Dressing

These types of sessions fall into two different categories. The first type is with the client who feels humiliated by having his masculinity robbed from him and having the "tables turned on him," as with slut training and maid training, and the second is with the client who becomes aroused by becoming more in touch with his feminine nature, as with full transformations. They may seem alike, but they are complete opposites! In the first session, the focus is more upon humiliation, and often, the punitive effect of putting a man in female clothing, while in the second, the focus is upon making the client feel good about becoming more feminine, and therefore, more divine.

Fetish Clothing

Remember that even if a client has contacted you for a kidnapping session, your clothing, personal presentation, and footwear are a VERY IMPORTANT element of the session. The appropriate clothing and footwear is essential to create the mood and state of arousal in the bottom.

Other common clothing fetishes
- Latex, Leather, or Shiny clothing fetish - If you look like you came straight out of a sci-fi movie or perhaps like Xena the warrior princess, this is ideal. The more futuristic and out of this world you appear, the better.
- Latex glove worship - especially opera or elbow length gloves
- Workout attire - crop tops, tiny tight bike shorts, yoga pants, and running shoes
- Tight jeans or Daisy Dukes - well fit so they show off your curves
- Lingerie, especially panties and stockings. Traditional, conservative satin full coverage panties, full length nude color nylons, and cuban foot thigh high stockings are common requests.

As a footnote, I would like to say that these are only the most commonly requested types of sessions. There are infinitely more variations on all of these themes, and no two sessions are exactly alike. In addition, the lingo, or slang, used to describe certain activities often changes over time, and there might be multiple slang terms that describe the same action.

Equipment

Common types of equipment and supplies you should be familiar with. I have put together this list of basic equipment with the intention of educating new Dominas who are just beginning their foray into BDSM. To some extent, a good Domme is only as good as the quality of her equipment, as well as her expertise! As you gain experience and develop your style, you will also slowly accumulate a nice array of equipment. Buy quality equipment that you will use over years and many happy hours of sessions.

General

Non latex medical gloves - use when applying genital bondage, when bottom may have contagious skin conditions or other communicative disease, when doing medical play, or at any other time when you want to avoid contact with blood or bodily fluids. Gloves are also very useful for cleaning up soiled equipment after the session and are a staple of any well equipped play space. Remember that some clients may be allergic to latex! At a minimum, have some non latex versions of gloves and condoms available in the case of latex allergies.

Cleaning supplies - As specified in the equipment care chapter, you will need to have your 90% alcohol, 1:10 bleach solution, and wood cleaner, and leather cleaner (wipes work great, and are convenient, but saddle soap is fine as well.) You may also want some other additional cleaners for the floor. Antibacterial wipes are also really handy and come in small travel packs for outcalls.

Paper towels and Baby Wipes - Paper towels are used not only for cleaning up various spills, but are also useful to have to you wipe your hands, and to use as "clean fields" for medical scenarios. Also, I noticed that germaphobes and men from some very conservative religious sects prefer to use paper towels after showering than machine washed towels. Baby wipes are useful to provide to your sub to clean themselves off after the session as well.

Pet pads or hospital style absorbent pads - These are used at any time you want to prevent   messes from liquid play. Will you be spitting red wine into your subs face? Are you planning an elaborate wax play scene? Will your sub be wetting his own panties so that you can humiliate him? Place a nice sized pet training pad over the floor or other area that you want to protect. It's always a good idea to avoid carpets, sofas, or other plush surfaces if you will be doing something like this.

Candles - Candles are not only an important part of your ambience, they are also useful to mask the odors of sweat after the session. I personally prefer to use LED rechargeable candles and burn incense, but the equipment that you choose is up to you. Candles are certainly easy to come by, relatively inexpensive, and easy to pack for an outcall or hotel session.

Incense - optional, but certainly a nice touch to burn before and after a session.

Rubber Bands - used as an aid to put on equipment such as cock rings, humblers, and donut shapes weights for CBT. They can also be used with chopsticks for a homemade CBT device.

Twine - Jute twine is sometimes used for CBT, but it is also very useful to have on hand to make emergency repairs, secure equipment to be packed in your suitcase. You can also use mason's twine to make single-tail crackers, as well as make repairs and secure equipment, but don't use mason's twine for CBT, because it frays and is very difficult to remove.

EMT safety scissors - These are an absolute MUST for any good Domme to have, and you should never do any kind of rope bondage, including CBT, without having a pair of safety scissors. They also come in handy to cut various other things during your sessions, so make sure that you buy a good quality pair.

Condoms - Yes, although it is true that as a Pro-Dominatrix, you will not be having sex with your clients, condoms are useful to have. Condoms can be placed over the penis of your sub to prevent accidental seminal fluid discharge, to place over toys, and even to cover phallic gags for your germaphobic subs. I generally opt for flavored, unlubricated condoms since they will be primarily used as barriers for non-sexual use, and I prefer to order them online from http://condomdepot.com so that I can maximize my savings while minimizing my need to run out the the drugstore.

A "Dirty Bag" - This is especially important for outcalls and traveling. You will want to keep a sturdy large trash bag or a specially designed waterproof bag for laundry to isolate your dirty ropes, cross dressing lingerie, and other equipment that needs to be specially cleaned from your clean equipment. If you forget to pack your dirty bag, you can use doubled up plastic grocery bags, hotel laundry bags, and store bought trash bags in a pinch. Make sure to tie them securely to prevent any dirty equipment from falling out in transition.

Mini flashlights - I use my mini flashlights in low light conditions to find items while cleaning up after the session, and also as an aide to help unlock handcuffs. Remember, you will be in top space (an exhilarating state of mind) and you may also need to decompress. Take all measures necessary to make the small things you need to do after the session a little easier.

Baby monitors with cameras - These are not really commonly used by Dommes, but might be useful if you are doing a long session involving fantasy "abandonment." This will allow you to monitor your sub's breathing and movement while still feeding the fear that your sub craves from being left alone in a precarious situation.

Bondage

Collar and Leash - The act of putting a collar on a submissive is one of the very first things that you will do to establish your dominance, both mentally and physically, in your sub. You may use leather fetish collars, posture collars, electronic bark collars, or simply a piece of smooth chain with no rough edges held together with a biner as your collar. Collars tend to get lost easily, so it is a good idea to have a few spares available. Collars and leashes can be found easily at pet stores as well as kinky supplier boutiques. Body harnesses are the full body version of a collar, and can be made of leather, chain, or tied with rope. Collars are intended not only as a sign of ownership, but as a way to easily control, bind, and submit your bottom to your desires.

Biners- There are a whole variety of industrial strength clips that you can use to secure your sub into place. Quick links, spring snap carabiner links, s-links, eye-bolt snaps, are just some of the types of binding links that you can find at your local hardware store. The most commonly used biners are called snap-link carabiners, and have a spring link opening that allows you to quickly click them onto cuffs, spreader bars, or bondage furniture and secure your sub into place. Be aware that biners are designed to carry various weights/loads, and that the type of biner that you use to anchor an arm or leg to a chair will likely not be strong enough to do a partial or complete suspension. Look on the packaging and take note of the load bearing capacity of your biner before you begin to use it.

Rope - Whether you use hemp, which is a favorite of Shibari lovers, poly blend found at your local hardware store, or cotton decorator's rope really depends upon your preference and the type of bondage that you will be doing. It goes without saying that you will need to have some training in bondage to know which ropes will fit your needs, and that not all ropes are adequate for heavy loads under tension. Soft cotton ropes are fine for light bondage such as a hand or leg double column tie, or perhaps a comfortable body harness that can be worn beneath the clothing. Cut your rope into 10-15 foot lengths for short ties (arms and legs) and 20-35 feet for body harnesses and more complicated ties.

Shoelaces or Twine - These are mainly used for CBT. Shoelaces are strong, easy to find, and washable, and therefore reusable! Shoelaces are also much more comfortable for light CBT, but can also be tied tight for heavier masochists. Twine is more uncomfortable on the skin, should be used for heavier masochists, and used once and thrown away after use.

Duct tape - You'd be surprised at how much great bondage equipment you can find at the 99 cent store! Duct tape is great for kidnapping scenes not only to tape over the mouth but also as a speedy way to bind your sub's arms and legs. Expert escape artists will usually get out of duct tape, but it is great for 75% of subbies who *don't want* to escape from their bondage. Duct tape should be cut off with EMT safety scissors after the scene, and removed with care unless your sub enjoys having his hair ripped out methodically and agonizingly while being released from bondage. Duct tape is also a useful thing to have on hand to repair plastic packing bins and mark places on the floor for your sub to stand on, among other things.

Saran wrap or shrink wrap - Used for "mummification" and restrictive bondage, but exercise extreme caution when used over the face. Never block both airways with anything other than your hands or another body part.

Metal cuffs/shackles - Real detective handcuffs can be purchased online, are difficult to escape from, and easy to apply, but hard to remove! Keep multiple copies of those little keys, and make sure they are on a huge, brightly colored or glow in the dark key chain. I keep one key in my purse at all times on my extra key ring, just in case I loose the other two copies that I keep in my bondage gear bag. Also, it may be useful to have a mini-flashlight on your keychain to help uncuff after the session.

While detective cuffs are great, it is nice to have BDSM specific shackles. They are designed for more comfortable long term wear, and often have nice features like small holes where tiny locks can be placed. As you become more established, buy good quality equipment because to a certain extent, your effectiveness as a Domme depends upon the variety and quality of equipment that you keep.

Leather cuffs - leather cuffs are the only kind of bondage device that should be used on delicate wrists and ankles for suspension. Leather cuffs are probably the most common types of cuffs used by BDSM enthusiasts because they are comfortable and quick and easy to apply. Suspension cuffs are a special type of leather cuff that have straps or handgrips for your sub to hold on to while they are suspended. These come in both the hand and foot versions.

Velcro cuffs - These are inexpensive and also quick and easy to apply. They may be preferable in outcall situations in which you have limited space, or for play parties where you might be worried about losing or damaging your expensive leather equipment.

Leather straps - For some scenes, like kidnapping or other types of roughing up fun, you don't want to waste too much time making perfect basket weaves or intricate ornamental knots with rope; you simply want to get your masochist pig bottom restrained so that you can torture him! In this instance, leather straps and belts can be useful, and of course, will delight the fetishist who loves leather and metal hardware in all of us!

Bungee cords - Can be used in a similar fashion to leather straps. Really great if you have bondage furniture with o-rings already in place.

Spreader bars- Great to have if you are traveling and can't take your St Andrew's cross with you. These are designed to keep your sub's ankles and wrists from touching, making them more vulnerable to torture. You can also use shorter spreader bars for behind the back wrist binding for less flexible subs, and with the right type of cuffs, can also be used on the legs above the knees, as well as the upper arms. Spreader bars are easy to make from wooden dowels and screw eyes found at hardware stores, and also come in adjustable length metal versions.

Hoods - Come in various types of material from spandex, to latex/rubber, PVC, and leather. Leather hoods are probably the most popular, and generally the ones with attached blindfolds, zip mouth, or gags are commonly chosen. Latex style balloon hoods are a favorite among subs who enjoy sensory deprivation and breath play. Use caution when using these types of hoods and monitor your sub at all times. Remember, they don't have to know you are watching!

Gags - All kinds of gags are available at your local kinky supplier, including bit style, 0-ring, dental retractors, phallic gags (great for humiliation and sissy sessions) and of course, the iconic ball gag. Ball gags are incredibly easy to make at home using a good quality plastic ball, a power drill, and some leather cord.

Blindfolds - Blindfolds are a very important part of the way you will take control, and is a very quick way to increase the suspense in a scene. A blindfold can be something as simple as a bandana from the army surplus supply, a silk scarf, or even a free sleep mask from your last cross country flight. You can find sleep masks at dollar stores, drugstores, and nice apothecaries, and of course, if you prefer leather and sheepskin, your local kinky supplier. Keep in mind that blindfolds are one of the most easily misplaced items in your inventory because of it's size and lightweight quality.

Forced intox masks or mouthpieces - Great for smoking sessions and other kinds of forced intox. They are also incredibly humiliating and a great way to torture a sub who cannot take intense pain, but wants to have his limits pushed.

Stockade - A medieval style wooden hinged gate that locks over the head and arms of the submissive. Stockades can be large pieces of furniture, but can also be a smaller piece that can be worn around the neck and fits over the wrists of the submissive prisoner.

Vises - Anything that is snapped together, on hinges, or secured with screws and is used to crush and constrict would be considered a vice. Humbler devices and ball crushing plates are examples of these.

Torture/Sado-Masochism

Clamps - You will want to have various types of clamps for nipple torture, CBT, and use all over the body for masochistic sessions. Adjustable clamps on chains are great for nipples which are durable and inseparably chained together for convenience. They are also great for leading subs around by their nipples, if you attach a leash to a small biner attached to the chain. Clover clamps are good for heavy nipple torture, and clothespins and modified industrial clamps are safe to use and easily found at local places around the neighborhood. An experienced kinkster can show you how to adjust the springs on industrial clamps so that they grip with less force.

Clothespins can be found at any dollar or drug store and are inexpensive and disposable.

Crops - Although the riding crop is the iconic tool of the Dominatrix, you can also use lightweight small leather paddles and leather slappers instead of crops. Crops are great to hit with when you cannot use heavy pressure, and are especially useful for CBT.

Floggers - A good flogger is an essential for any kinkster, and will most likely be your first major expense (or gift, if you have personal slaves who like to pamper you.) Stay away from cheap plastic floggers and go with heavy suede, leather, or some other natural skin. Lightweight handles are preferable to heavy metal ones, especially if you get a lot of sensation pigs who love to be flogged in 30 minute stretches. **Note:** Cats (or cat of nine tails) are similar to floggers   in that they have many tails, but they are usually made of leather and have small knots or sometimes even metal parts on the ends. Cats and rubber floggers are stingy and will leave heavy markings, while floggers are generally thuddy, more sensual, and better for extended percussive play.

Straps/belts - straps and belts are common requests for domestic discipline. A simple men's leather belt worn with dress pants is easy to use, while a Russian razor strap will require some training and skill to use well. The equipment you choose depends upon your level of training and experience and also your preferences. There are also variations of belts such as traditional english quirts which you can find at a quality kinky supplier.

Hairbrush, wooden kitchen spoon or spatula - these are also commonly used for domestic discipline.

Paddles - for Ladies just starting out, I would recommend having at least one light to medium weight leather paddle of very good quality, and one larger sized heavy fraternity style wooden paddle.. For lighter punishments, you can use ping pong paddles found at big box or sporting goods stores, or well made leather paddles with or without fur on the reverse side to soothe the sting after the punishment has been administered.

Canes - bamboo canes are the most popular, but you can also find plastic versions that are   much easier to clean and maintain, and generally can be used for a longer time. Bamboo canes are easy to make from gardening stakes if they are properly cut, sanded, and conditioned.

Single tails - Who has not conjured up the iconic vision of a stiletto boot clad Dominatrix cracking her bullwhip? The use of single tails are a great way to elicit the fear response in your sub, even if you do not hit them with it! They can be used lightly, or cracked with a vengeance over a heavy masochist's back. Single tails cause extreme pain to the lucky (or unfortunate) soul on the receiving end of the whip, but they can draw blood and even cause permanent scars. You will need a substantial amount of practice before you can competently use a single tail on a live person. First, do target practice with pillows, sheets of paper, or small stuffed animals at home until you develop proficiency, and make sure not to "wrap" the whip around the side of the body. Dragon tails and flicker whips are variations of single tails that do not crack (break the sound barrier.)

Suction Devices - Whether you use plastic vacuum pumps, Chinese fire cups, snake bite kits, or other adult specialty products depends upon your training and preference.

Vampire gloves - a great toy for sensation pigs and bottoms who cannot handle heavy pain, vampire gloves are the perfect combination of silky softness and the tender bite of metal. Don't use them over open wounds or skin conditions, and be aware that they will snag on your expensive lingerie and silk stockings if you are not careful.

Medical

Because you will need special training and mentorship to do medical play, I will simply go into the two electrical devices which are commonly used by Pro-Dommes. Medical play can be extremely intense and rewarding, but it carries some serious risks of infection to your sub, so you should make sure to get proper mentorship from other Pro-Dominas or kinky medical professionals in your area who can teach you the most important safety precautions to be aware of before this type of play.

Medical Paraphernalia - It is a great idea to have a stethoscope, notepad, thermometers,   various types of scopes, gloves, and other items that are used in medical settings. Some of these might be props, such as medical posters or diagrams, while others will be items used for play. Make sure you understand how to clean your equipment and take precautions to prevent spread of infection. Use approved barriers and coverings for thermometers and other equipment whenever possible.

Violet wands - Also known as "high frequency machines," violet wands are used by aestheticians to kill bacteria on their client's faces after performing facials. They generate an electrical impulse which travels in a closed circuit pattern, meaning that it will make contact with your skin and then travel back to the wand itself, thus the electrical impulse will not be transmitted through the body. They are safe to use even by amateurs as long as care is taken not to break the glass tube components of the wand, and are safe to use all over the body, even on the scalp, earlobes, and lips, but don't use the wands near the eyes!

Tens Units - These medical devices commonly used by chiropractors generate an electrical impulse that travels through the body. *NEVER* use a tens unit in such a way that the electrical impulse travels through the chest cavity. Electrical impulses generated by tens units can disrupt cardiac rhythms, even in healthy individuals, and improper use can lead to heart arrhythmias and even cardiac arrest. Tens units pads and conducting devices can be used on arms and legs and the lower body safely, as long as no pads are placed over the chest or upper back area. Also avoid placing pads in such a way that the electrical impulse must travel through the core of the body, such as one pad on a hand and another one on an opposite leg. Never use tens units on any bottom who has a pacemaker or who has a history of heart attacks or arrythmias.

Furniture

What furniture you maintain or have access to depends upon whether you work from home or a dungeon space, the size of your space, and the common types of sessions that you accept. Here are a few pieces of furniture that you should consider.

A sturdy wooden or metal chair

For rope or even cuff bondage, you will want a very strong chair that can safely hold a struggling sub as long as you keep him bound. It does not necessarily need to be a chair designed for bondage, but it should have lots of anchor points, which will allow rope to pass through, or maybe even bars or openings which can accommodate standard biners. If you are handy, or have a sub who is, you can also install some o-ring hooks (called "screw eyes" at your local hardware store) that you can put biners into.

Bondage beds

If you work from home, consider getting a very sturdy metal or wood framed bed with lots of anchor points for rope and cuffs. If you will be routinely playing on your bed, also consider getting a waterproof mattress cover so that you can avoid any accidental spills that might soil your mattress. As with your chair, it is possible to install 0-ring hooks (screw eyes) into the frame of your bed so that you can quickly snap in your cuffed sub, making them ready for the most delectable kinds of torture. If you don't have a bondage bed, you will find that it is fairly easy to modify a secondhand massage table by putting large carabiners around the legs to use as anchor points, and fastening a few leather straps or pieces of rope to the middle portion of the table which will allow the core of your bottoms body to be secured to the table.

If you work from a dungeon space, you will most likely have access to bondage beds, spanking horses, stockades, mechanized trailer winches, and St. Andrew's crosses which are especially designed for bondage. Well equipped spaces sometimes even have vacuum beds, coffins, medical exam tables, and inversion crosses or tables, as well as cages and jail cells.

Start slowly!

It will take time to accumulate all of your equipment! Your best bet is to find a few nice basic pieces from your local kinky boutique to start with, and raid your local hardware store and dollar store for as much as you can find when you first start out. More than likely, many of your bottoms will offer to bring their own equipment to play with, or even to gift you some nice pieces if they take a liking to you. Submissive men love to please, and are likely to be very excited about the possibility of taking you on a kinky shopping trip for equipment that you use together after the trip.

Equipment is very important, but creativity is your most important asset. Keep talking to your bottoms while you play with them. Remember, ultimately they are coming to see *YOU*, and your charm, personality, and creativity will carry the session.

More Tips for Equipment

Some pieces of BDSM equipment are not always the easiest to figure out how to use intuitively. Cock rings, crushing plates, and humblers definitely fall into this category. I was lucky enough as a lifestyle Domme to be able to have friends and confidants who gave me plenty of tips to make putting on equipment safely much easier, but not all Ladies are this lucky.

Cock Rings
To begin placing on a cock ring (or the bottom plate of a crushing vise) first, find a wide rubber band and place it around the base of both the penis and scrotum, making sure that it fits snugly (you may have to double it over to do this.) Feel quickly to make sure that both testes are inside the scrotum, since sometimes they have a tendency to drift up into the pubic region. You may have to use a downwards swiping motion with your hand to cause the testacle to descend before you are able to rubber band it off to prevent it from ascending again. After the rubber band is in place, put the penis through the ring. While holding the ring with one hand, slowly and carefully begin pulling the skin of one half of the scrotum through the ring with the other hand. If the testacle is small, it may come right through the ring with the skin, but most of the time, you will need to give it a small push from the back in order to get it in. After you have one ball in, repeat this process with the other side of the scrotum. Finally, when the ring is completely on, cut off the rubber band with EMT safety scissors.

Humblers and Donut Shapes Weights

Humblers are so compelling for submissive men, and many of them dream of wearing one to please their Lady even for just one hour, however, they are often much more difficult to wear than they immediately appear. The trick to putting on a humbler with minimum whining from your sub is to make sure that the delicate skin of the scrotum does not get caught in the device while you are locking it over. The secret to getting this done quickly is to use a wide rubber band to make sure that the scrotal skin is protected. You may need to double over the rubber band in order to compress the ball sac enough to fit into your device. After you have locked on the humbler or screwed on the weights, you can then cut off the rubber band using EMT safety scissors.

How to Put on a Cockring

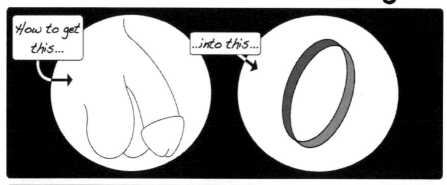

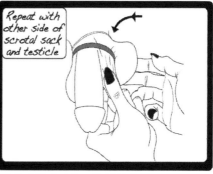

Equipment Care

Your various pieces of equipment are your work tools! Take good care of them and they will serve you well for years to come.

Cleaners

Most equipment care can be taken care of with four types of cleaners.

90% alcohol in a spray bottle- Spray bottles of this are sold at most major drugstore chains   and also local mom and pop places. This percentage of alcohol is known to kill 99% of all bacteria, is gentle enough to be used on your hands as a sanitizer, and a fine mist can be used for leather goods and most delicate items, including feathers, and even wood. Wood clothespins should be opened and sprayed on the inside surface of the clamp that has come into contact with the skin.

1:10 bleach and water solution - This is a healthcare setting approved cleaning ratio, and it is adequate enough to clean up blood spills in a hospital setting, and can be made using one part bleach and ten parts water. Use bleach with caution, however. It should not be used on leather, wood, or cloth equipment because it will bleach the color out of these items. Use bleach for metal and plastic objects, and anything that accidentally comes into contact with blood and bodily fluids. Metal and plastic clamps should be opened and sprayed on the inside surface of the clamp that has come into contact with skin. Bleach solution is not appropriate for cleaning medical equipment that is designed for single use and meant to be thrown away after use.

Saddle Soap, Leather Cleaning Wipes or Spray - After spritzing your leather with a very fine mist of 90% alcohol, it is good to clean and condition it every so often with leather specific cleaners. Although alcohol is very gentle, repeated use will dry and discolor your leather if you do not condition it. I would recommend conditioning at least once per week with frequent use of a toy, or once a month with less frequently used toys. Don't forget to condition your leather clothing and shoes as well! This is a good task to give to a slave/sub who is desperate to serve you. Suede can be cleaned with a special spray designed for suede, but from my experience, you're better off just sticking with the alcohol.

Murphy's Wood Oil Soap/Natural Wood Cleaner - Wood can be cleaned quickly with a quick spritz of alcohol, but wood should also be cleaned with special wood cleaner every so often. Bleach will strip enamel, wood treatments and stains, and weaken the wood, so don't use bleach unless your wood has come into contact with blood, which does happen every so often with bamboo canes. In general though, bamboo canes are fairly easy to come by and make at home, so I opt to throw out bamboo canes, wood clothespins, and inexpensive items that have been contaminated with blood. Clean your wood paddles lovingly with wood conditioner about as often as you would condition leather, that is, once a week to once a month. Remember that since these wood items are coming into contact with human flesh, you will want a natural cleaner that is free of most toxins and chemicals. This, again, is a good task for subs and slaves.

Cavicide - Cavicide is a broad spectrum antiseptic cleaner used in medical settings, and is used by Dommes who do lots of medical play. For most purposes, bleach and water is sufficient. You will not need to use Cavicide unless you have been trained in certain types of medical play. Keep in mind, you should *NEVER* reuse needles, catheters, or anything which is designed for single use. Ideally, you will want to have an autoclave for scopes, dilators, plugs, and other commonly used S&M medical equipment made of surgical steel that can withstand high heat. Occasionally though, you may want to wipe off your exam table with Cavicide in addition to the bleach/water solution.

Rope

Rope will come in long lengths and will need to be cut down and "finished" at the ends to prevent fraying. You will need at least four short lengths (10-15 feet) for arm and leg single and double column ties, and longer lengths (25- 30 feet) for body harnesses and more complicated bondage. What type of rope you choose and how much of it to get depends upon your training, preferred style, and how you incorporate rope play into your sessions. If you generally only tie someone's hands quickly, or perhaps a leg to a chair, keep your lengths short. Nothing is more annoying to both Domme and sub that long lengths of rope that must be pulled through existing rope work again and again, creating rope burns for the rope bottom. Keep in mind that hemp has the lowest "burn speed," which is defined as the amount of movement necessary to create irritation and abrasions on the rope bottoms' skin.

Hemp rope is a favorite among Shibari as well as American and Eclectic style bondage enthusiasts for its durability and ability to hold a knot, and it holds the bends and turns that are commonly found in Japanese style Shibari without slipping, however, most types of hemp cannot be washed in a machine. Remember that bacteria thrive in a *dark moist* environment and that a **dry, well lit by sunlight** space will generally be free of most types of bacteria. Hemp can be effectively "cleaned" by being placed loosely coiled so as to allow maximum oxygen through the material in bright sunlight, and then isolated (not used) for two weeks. Most bacteria and even viruses will not survive on dry objects for that amount of time. So, rule number one of keeping your rope and other equipment clean is to keep it *dry* and well ventilated.

Cotton and poly blend style ropes found at hardware stores, as well as cloth blindfolds, gags, and bandanas, can be thrown in the washing machine and then air dried. You will need to tie your ropes in a daisy chain or fold them over a few times until they are no longer than two feet and then tie an overhand knot in the center before putting them in the wash. The common wisdom is that you need to put your ropes in a laundry bag, but I have found this unnecessary if the ropes are securely tied. Wash your ropes *cold* and never put them in the electric dryer because this will cause the material to fray, and poly blend rope material is heat sensitive. My personal rule for washing rope is that If it comes into contact with bodily fluid, is used to tie genitals or run across a rope bottom's bare anus, or comes into contact with blood, it gets washed. Rope used to do simple hand and feet ties gets tied and reused.

All types of rope will need to be "finished." For hemp and cotton rope, take a needle and thread and run it through the end of the rope a few times to anchor it, and then wrap the thread a few times around the circumference of the rope. Then run the needle back through the rope a few more times to anchor it yet again, and tie off the finished end. Poly blend rope with synthetic fibers as well as paracord found at army surplus stores can be finished with the heat of a flame from a candle or a lighter. The heat from the flame will cause the synthetic fibers to melt into the rope, effectively stopping the rope from fraying. You may want to carefully pinch the melted end of the rope between two pieces of cardboard after it has cooled a little for a smooth tip. A discussion of how to finish rope, as well as other useful information pertaining to rope bondage, can be found in Jay Wiseman's Erotic Bondage Handbook.

Rubber and Latex Clothing

Rubber and latex clothing needs to be cleaned occasionally. The best way to clean it is to rinse it with lukewarm water with a bit of dish soap in it. Swirl the garment quickly and then rinse it liberally with lots of cold water so that you will not have any soapy residue left, and then hang it to dry. When it is fully dry, you will need to powder both the outside and inside surface and place the item in a ziplock bag until next use. Unpowered latex surfaces will stick together and are very difficult to separate, and you will need a delicate hand with your freshly washed garment. As you carefully peel away the surfaces, sprinkle some baby powder on the inside. A little actually goes quite a long way, especially if you rub the powder across the surface with either your hand or the opposite surface of the garment. Anecdotally, I have heard of people using cornstarch to powder their garments, however, be advised that you may get mold growing in your favorite outfit if you don't wear it frequently! Remember also that rubber and latex will dry out in low humidity environments, so make sure to keep them in ziplock bags when fully dry to protect them.

PVC Clothing

PVC needs to be hand washed in a similar fashion to latex clothing, but the difference is that you do not need to powder it. PVC is much thicker, and it can take a long time to air dry, especially in humid environments. It should not be left out in the sun for more than a day because it will peel and crack. I once ruined one of my favorite PVC catsuits because I could not get it to dry one summer, and then forgot about it as it was drying outside. Wash your PVC, rubber, and latex only when absolutely necessary, and keep the garments dry.

Legal Issues & Ethics

As a professional, it is understood that you will abide by a code of ethics. You will need to properly obtain consent from your clients, take reasonable measures to protect their privacy, and take every precaution possible to protect their physical safety during your sessions.

Obtaining Consent

Generally, an initial contact will take place via email or by phone, and in normal circumstances, your client will be fully mentally alert and not under the influence of controlled substances or alcohol. Although under most circumstances for light sessions verbal consent given by the bottom should be adequate, for heavier sessions, it is preferable to obtain written consent for BDSM activity prior to the session. This could be an email with the client's description of activities or fantasies that he would like to play out, or sometimes it might take the form of a questionnaire filled out by the bottom.

While for light sessions verbal consent is adequate, if the client arrives drunk, under the influence of prescription or illicit drugs, or perhaps has a mental illness that impairs their judgement, ascertaining whether you are obtaining a genuine consent can be difficult. If you suspect that your client is impaired for some reason, you should exercise extreme caution in engaging in risky or extreme S&M, especially if you have never seen them before. Determining whether your client is able to give consent is highly subjective, and has legal as well as personal ramifications. Your clients will not generally take you to court because they prefer for their sexual preferences to remain private, however, there are some legal conditions that you should know about in order to be an informed provider of this kind of intimate service.

Safe Words and Safe Signals

A commercial Domme will generally allow the use of a safe word such as "red" or "mercy." Some bottoms will decline the opportunity to use a safe word, and in that case, use your best judgement. In cases in which a bottom may be hooded or gagged and unable to speak, I generally will give my bottom a "safe signal" so that they can alert me that they need to stop. Usually, this will be something like a wrestling style tap for close contact activities like smothering or breath play sessions, or multiple stomps of the foot or repeated hand flashing in the case that they are in bondage while gagged or being single tailed. The agreement upon a safe word or signal is am important part of ensuring that full consent is obtained and that play is mutually desired and enjoyable.

Legal Issues

In most states, BDSM and fetish activity falls into a legal "gray area." Most activities are not specifically illegal, but they not entirely legally protected either. In general, most types of sado-masochism, including CBT, are not considered sex acts, and are difficult to prosecute in court. Some states have transparent laws that clearly describe what constitutes a sex act, for instance, exchange of bodily fluids (generally considered to be genital secretions,) or insertion of body parts, fingers, or objects into the anus or vagina. Other states have very unclear, ambiguous language in their laws. In some states, nudity is not considered a violation of the law, while in other states, you would need to be registered and bonded to provide any type of adult service. The most common activity that generally results in arrests of Dominatrixes would be insertion of objects, including plugs and strap-ons, into the anus of the client. You might also be fined or arrested for participating in certain types of medical play, but this is rare.

Remember also that although it will generally be of legal benefit to you to have written documentation of consent such as email and written slave applications, legally, no one can consent to a beating. I have not heard of bottoms suing Dominas for cuts, scrapes and bruises or more major trauma such as varicoceles resulting from CBT, however, there have been a few prominent cases of Dominas who were not properly trained charged with manslaughter for the deaths of submissives under their supervision. Use your best judgement and err on the side of caution. Stopping short of a very intense act does not make you any less of a Bad Ass Bitch.

Protect Yourself
Don't go into clear detail about what you do on the phone. Allow your caller to talk to you about their fantasies, and allow them to say what they wish on the phone. Do not promise any particular service for money. Tribute is accepted for your time, and *only* your time. Accept tribute only *after* your session, and don't promise any specific activity before the session. You are a Goddess and your bottom/slave/submissive is there to please *YOU*. Although it is a risk to accept your tribute after your session, I know from experience that if you practice with integrity, heart, and passion, your bottom will not deny you your deserved tribute.

Screening Your Calls and Email
Many Ladies will put a disclaimer in their emails, explaining that they don't respond to explicit requests, and that their tribute is in exchange for their time only. In general, however, in you can allow the client to say anything they like in the email or call, but it is what you say that is more

important, especially in phone conversations. Don't promise activities which involve exchange of bodily fluids, insertion of objects into the anus or vagina, or any type of manual/digital sex (hand jobs or fingering.) Generally, it is best to be very discreet about your activities, however, some clients will not want to see you without a reasonable amount of information so that they can gauge your level of experience, and also so they can make a judgement about your personality and compatibility with them. Use your judgement and don't promise services that you know are illegal.

Medical Concerns

Before planning a scene with a new sub, it is important to take into account the health and current medical state of your new bottom. Following is a brief list of the most common health concerns that you should be aware of when interviewing your client. Keep in mind that this is not a complete list, and that medical status of each person should be considered individually. There are certainly other issues that you should consider which may not be listed here, but the following are things that you should always ask about before a session. Asking about health and medical issues is the responsible thing to do, and all of the best and top Pro Dommes have had training in negotiating play with respect to medical issues.

Movement Restrictions - It is very common that your sub might have sustained some past injury which results in some sort of pain or movement restrictions, such as anterior-cruciate ligament and rotator cuff tears or strains, or spinal joint injuries. In lay language, any kind of arthritis, ligament or tendon injury, or bone misalignment which can cause pain should be considered before planning tight bondage, partial or full suspension, or sustained crawling.

Circulatory Problems - Does your client have diabetes or any other issue that influences blood circulation? If so, use caution before applying tight limb or genital bondage or placing them in any sort of restrictive, tight devices which might more easily lead to injury in these people.

Bruising - Some individuals have a propensity to bruise more easily than others, and some may be on blood thinners such as Heparin or Warfarin, or even over the counter medicine such as aspirin which may cause large bruises. In addition, in the case of accidental cuts, it will take longer than average for their blood to clot, and you will need to place pressure on the area and bandage it before continuing play.

Heart Problems - Heart problems can lead to dizziness and fainting. Find out if your client has ever had heart arrhythmias or heart attacks before playing, or if they have a pacemaker. Don't use tens units over the thorax or upper back of anyone with a pacemaker, because it may interfere with the device's ability to promote normal heart rhythms. (Violet wands are different, because the wand itself makes energy flow in a closed circuit pattern, and it does not flow through the entire body the way that a tens signal does, but to be safe, avoid use of any electro-play devices over the chest of someone with a pacemaker.) With some clients, you may not want to place them in bondage in a standing position, or suspend them facing down in case they faint. In the case of the downward facing suspension, the weight of your bottom's own body might prevent him from breathing properly if he passes out. Avoid inversions (positions in which they are upside down) for more than a few seconds at a time until you are able to determine their level of tolerance for this kind of play.

High/Low Blood Pressure - Both high and low blood pressure can be associated with increased incidence of dizziness or fainting. Take the same precautions that you would use for someone with a heart problem, and do not bind them for long periods standing or hanging facing downwards, and especially avoid inverted suspensions in which they are upside down. Reclining or laying a bottom flat, such as on an exam table or bondage bed, is safe for those with blood pressure concerns, but be aware that the sudden change in blood pressure that results from your client getting up after laying down for a long period of time may also cause dizziness. Instruct them to get up slowly after removing all rope or bondage equipment and watch them for a minute to make sure that they are okay.

Blood Borne Disease - Most people are aware that precautions need to be taken with play partners who are HIV positive, but they probably don't realize that the person with HIV is actually at more risk of injury or infection during a play session than their healthy partner. Of course, you will want to be very careful to prevent the spread of blood or any other bodily fluid in this case. You may want to place a condom over their penis to prevent any accidental emission of seminal fluid that might pose a contamination risk to yourself or others, and of course, take special care to avoid blood letting. Be aware though, that your risk of contracting HIV is actually much lower than your bottom's risk of becoming sick from an infection due to your use of contaminated equipment. It goes without saying that you should only use single use, disposable medical devices and toys, and that you should make sure any corporal punishment equipment used on them is cleaned *before* as well as after use.

In most cases, the risk of the spread of Hepatitis C and even Hepatitis B in a play setting is much higher than the risks from HIV. Hep C is primarily blood borne and can be transmitted through shared needles and exchange of blood. Hep B can be transmitted through sweat and is more common than Hep C. Be very cautious in the case of cuts or any kind of blood spills, and make sure that you use your bleach solution to clean thoroughly in the case of any accidents.

Active Contagious Skin Conditions - Certain skin conditions, most commonly active shingles   and both oral and genital forms of herpes can present an infection risk to you, and also can shed the virus onto your equipment. It is best not to play with someone with active shingles, however, if you do you should use barriers (T-shirts, gauze covering) over the lesions to prevent spread of the virus. In the case of genital herpes, use medical exam gloves when applying twine or shoelace for genital bondage, and place a condom over the penis to prevent any kind of skin to skin contact. If possible, use equipment that is disposable, such as shoelaces, wooden kitchen utensils from dollars stores for discipline, wooden or plastic clothespins, and hardware store poly blend rope that can be replaced inexpensively. Use exam gloves when cleaning up after the session and make liberal use of your bleach solution when cleaning equipment. You may also want to isolate the equipment used for up to two weeks if possible, and make sure it is dry before using it again.

Breathing Conditions - Any sort of breathing condition, whether it be a chronic lung issue or a little cold which caused mucous or wheezing, should be considered before putting your bottom in gags that may make breathing difficult, hoods that cover the mouth or enough of the nostrils to prevent proper air flow, or tight bondage that restricts normal chest movement. There was a very high profile case of manslaughter pending against a Dominatrix who left a sub in a closet for hours with a straw taped into his mouth to breathe with. The sub quickly became unable to breathe and died before she went back to check on him. Be aware that even in completely healthy individuals, being placed reclining on their back with gags or other objects in their mouth may cause saliva to accumulate which may choke them or block their air passages. Even the use of forced intox masks and o-ring gags specifically designed for bdsm use can lead to choking if liquids are poured into the sub's mouth and he is not able to close his jaw enough to perform his normal swallowing reflex.

Allergies - Allergies, especially latex allergies, are important to be aware of since they will result in anaphylactic shock (elevated heart rate, breathing changes and difficulty, rashes or hives.) Don't wear latex clothing for your session if your client is allergic, and avoid food play with any substance that they are allergic to. The only way you will find out about allergens is to do a complete and comprehensive interview during your negotiation.

🐚 🐚 🐚

Have an investigator's eye! Does your bottom have a strange scar across their chest? Do they have a band-aid over one of their legs? Can you see a strange bump somewhere in their back that they didn't mention? It never hurts to ask about it, and it's perfectly ok to do so, even in the middle of a session, if necessary.

Have a plan of action that both you and your client put together in the case that a medical emergency happens during your session. It may be as simple as calling 911, or it might be to have an emergency contact number handy just in case. In most cases due to the privacy considerations of your sub, they will prefer to simply notify you that a medical problem exists and elect to have you call 911 in case of an emergency.

If possible, take a class in CPR and first aid, and get the basics down before taking sessions. You should know how to handle the most common first aid concerns, including small cuts and abrasions, minor burns, and how to respond in the case that a sub passes out or faints while in session with you. You may want to ask one of your regular subs to sponsor you for this kind of class, or at the minimum , you should maintain a well stocked first aid kit and have read some basic first aid information before ever taking a single session. Get a kindle version or paper issue of the American Red Cross First Aid Handbook for more information about first aid.

Aftercare

It often happens that small wounds, cuts, scrapes, or abrasions result from BDSM play, especially during corporal punishment scenes! The follow up treatment that a good Dominatrix provides for her bottoms is referred to as "aftercare." This may be something as simple as putting a small dab of anti-bacterial cream and a band-aid on a cut, or even providing a blanket and a warm cup of water to someone who has fainted. You will not always need to provide aftercare, and in most cases, such as in heavy bruising, you can instruct your bottom as to how to care for their wounds at home, in this case by placing cold packs over the area to minimize inflammation. It is usually enough to have the first aid materials on hand and to instruct your sub how to clean and cover their cuts and bruises.

Safety Issues

Aside from medical concerns, there are safety concerns that should be considered for all healthy individuals with regards to BDSM play.

The face - is one of the most delicate regions on the human body and is the location of the eyes, which are especially vulnerable to injury. Avoid percussive play other than face slapping on the face, and never use fire wands or place open flames near the face and hair.

The clavicle, sternum, and xiphoid process - These are known colloquially as the "collarbone," and "breast plate" and are vulnerable to being broken. It is okay to use floggers and any kind of implement that creates dispersed impact (pressure that is distributed rather than concentrated) and stingy sensations. While most newbies know enough not to use wooden paddles on the chest, some new Dominas don't consider trampling risks to this area. Don't walk over the collarbone or xiphoid process, the tiny bone at the base of the sternum which can be easily broken or misaligned.

The floating ribs - these are located both from the front and back of the body, and loosely cover the kidneys. Never punch, kick, or trample over the floating ribs. The kidneys are easily bruised and trauma to these vital and delicate organs can be extremely dangerous. Aside from the danger to the kidneys, the floating ribs are also easily broken.

Joints - Use caution around elbows, knees, wrists, ankles, and the small joints in the hands . Never apply percussive play over any joints on the extremities or neck, and when putting your sub in bondage, make sure that the cuffs or rope sits securely *above* or *below* the joints. Never trample over the joints from any direction. Joints can be easily misaligned and there are always major nerve and blood vessels passing through these areas.

Spine and Sacrum - The spine and triangular shaped bone right below it should never sustain anything other than dispersed impact from a flogger, or light sensory stimulation. Light, stingy impacts from singletails or even canes are okay, but avoid concentrated blows such as punches and kicks. The spine is especially vulnerable to becoming misaligned, having delicate spinal processes broken, and both the spine and sacrum are a dense nexus of important nerve pathways that can be damaged or become impinged.

Feet - Like hands, the feet are composed of many small and delicate joints, tendons, and ligaments. Although I get requests for bastinado sessions to the feet on occasion, the truth is that it is not safe to sustain repeated strong impacts with anything other than a lightweight bamboo cane, ruler, riding crop, or similar tool, to the feet. It is bad for the joints, but can also result in painful tendonitis that can make it difficult to walk while the area is inflamed.

The best places for intense punishments on the rear of the body are the buttocks below the sacrum (basically below the butt crack,) the upper legs above the knee and below the pubic bone, the thighs, and the upper back. All areas mentioned aside from the upper back can are well protected by thick muscle layers and can sustain heavy paddlings and deeper impacts. The upper back is a wonderful area for heavy flogging, canings, and whips from singletails.

Wooden Paddles should *only* be used on the gluteal (buttock) area and upper legs and thighs *period*. Never paddle any other area on the body with wood or any thick heavy object which has the potential to break bones or cause internal injury to delicate organs .

The best places to punish on the front of the body are the pectoral areas ("pecs") which are covered with dense thick musculature, and also the abdomen, and upper legs.   These areas can sustain heavier impacts, including controlled punching and controlled kicking, more safely than other areas.

When trampling, keep your weight on the safe for play areas, and avoid joints, spine, and bones vulnerable to breaking.

Color Codes for Illustration

Red - No heavy impacts, Thuddy percussive play, or trampling over this area. Light sensation play with feathers, Whartonburg wheels, and dispersed impact with floggers is okay.

White - use caution when trampling or punching. Best not to apply full body weight when trampling. No heavy impact play with paddles and heavy duty equipment.

Blue - Dense areas of musculature which are the best areas for all kinds of punishment. Use caution around body processes of the pelvis.

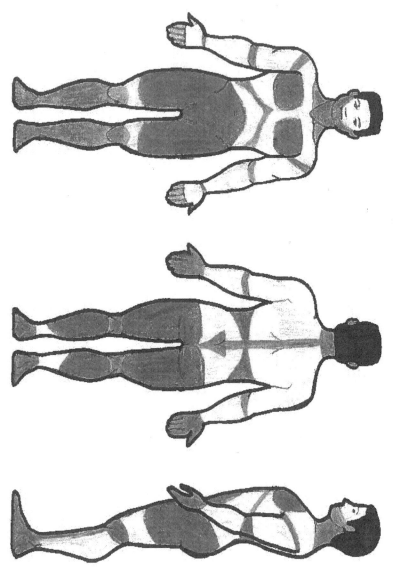

Advertising and Self Promotion

Pro-Dommes are well known personalities in the relatively small BDSM community. If you are really talented and skilled, or if you are not well trained or incompetent, word gets around pretty quickly. It will also be very obvious from the get go whether you are very experienced, or highly inexperienced. Your experience and talent is paramount, but don't underestimate the value of good advertising, marketing, and personal promotion. It is the advertising that will intrigue your prospective submissives, and your skills and talents that will keep them coming back to see you again and again. Let's walk through the basics of self promotion.

Photos, Website and Social Media

Aside from training (you should have a few months of training or switching before you ever post your first ad) one of the most important things you will need for effective self promotion are really amazing photographs. Your photos, your alluring bio, and your mystique are the hooks that will lure your prospective clients. You should plan on keeping a full portfolio and updating your photos at least once or twice a year. Many Dominas also do part time modeling for magazines, artistic projects, and film for pay. Your portfolio should be your chance to show off your most amazing, sexy, eye catching fetish outfits. Oftentimes, clients will call and request for you to wear particular outfits that they have seen in the photos, so be prepared to have that outfit handy if you are using photos of it for advertising.

If you are just starting out, one of the best ways to get photos for little or no cost is through modeling networking sites such as http://model mayhem.com , which allows anyone to post a free profile that takes about ten minutes to complete. Of course, the usual rules of caution apply. You may want to ask if you can bring a girlfriend (girlfriends are better received that boyfriends for male photographers) with you on your first shoot, and if the photographer is legit and professional, they should have no problem with this. Hopefully, you will get offers for TFP, also called PFT- Prints for Time) shoots, in which you offer your time for one or two hours and in exchange, you should get three to five touched up images or sometimes even a whole sessions worth of digitals on a disk, flash drive, or in a dropbox.

Your images are iconic representations of your personality, so choose those which represent who you most feel you are as a Domina. If you are more of a sensual Domme, choose softer, very feminine representations which evoke a feeling of luxuriousness. If you tend to be more of a heavy sadist, use shots which show you in a dark and ominous light. Fetish items and clothing, such as gas masks, latex garments, boots, stilettos, and dungeon furniture should be prominent, if possible, in your photos. At the minimum, you should have some equipment that you use nearby in the background.

Always maintain a very professional looking website with lots of photos of yourself, as well as a complete bio and activities that you enjoy. Blogs, Twitter, Instagram, and other social media are another great way to keep your subs and bottoms abreast of your recent travels, parties attended, projects participated in, and more, and it is a great way to get passive traffic and exposure. if you are cross linked appropriately and have the right meta tags embedded in your website description, it should be fairly easy to get several hundred to even thousands of hits every week.

Advertising

You will need to direct a sizable amount of your income towards advertising. The top sites to place advertisements are Backpage, Cityvibe, ErosGuide, OpenAdultDirectory and Pandemos. There are definitely other sites that you can use, however, from my years of experience I have found both through asking clients who actually show up and through my website analytics app that most of my hits and contacts have come from these few sites, as well as DickieVirgin, which is more of a link exchange than an advertising site. Generally, the lower cost ads will get you clients who will try to bargain with you, and the higher cost ads will allow higher end, sophisticated clientele to find you, however, much of your business and opportunities will come as a result of quality of your website, video clips posted online, word of mouth, and yes, fetish parties. Networking is another very important part of self promotion discussed in the next section.

Your ads need not be very lengthy, however, they should incite curiosity, showcase skills and talents that are unique to you, and portray you as a very responsible, well trained professional. Maintain an amazing website and always put a link to your website in your ads and your email signature. Your website is your own platform to tell the world all about what makes you amazing, and is a very important tool for networking as well.

Networking

Parties - Fetish parties are important ways to meet others in the kinky community. You may not get any direct sessions from attending parties, however, you will most likely meet photographers, fetish fashion designers, DJs, party hosts, and other Dominas who will offer you modeling, film, hostess, or other work opportunities if they like you, your look, and your personality. Always attend parties dressed to the nines in your best fetish gear, but don't go with over the top expectations. Have a good time, chat other people up, and observe other party goer's amazing bondage work or their well behaved submissives. Although it is true that some of my best opportunities have sprung from parties that I have attended, primarily, parties are for kinky community bonding and cutting loose!

Leather Groups - Leather groups are not only important for training and demonstrations, they are also really good ways to meet people. I met a long term sub who served me for several years until his unfortunate passing at a leather group training at a local BDSM club in a new area that I had moved to. Through him I was introduced to other people in the kinky community as well.

Events - Volunteering for events like Leather Pride Fundraiser is also a good way to meet people and learn about news and other events happening in the leather scene, and is also a good way to build a support network and give back to the community. Even today, members of the leather community still experience harassment, loss of their job, and other problems due to news of their private behavior going public to friends, family, and work associates.

Screening your calls and Email

I learned some very important sales techniques during a brief career in real estate that increased my productiveness and number of sessions by 150%. Your ability to get sessions is completely a function of how well you are able to create rapport on the phone, screen your calls, and make good use of your personal time. Remember, as a Pro-Domme, you are self employed, and how much you work and how well you are able to make kinky contacts depends not only upon your ability to market yourself, but also on how quickly you are able to gauge whether your caller is genuine in his intent to see you, or simply wasting your time. Please note that although I refer to the submissive men as "clients" in this section, it is very bad form refer to your sub male who tributes as a "client." You are providing a fantasy service, and as such, don't break the veil of the fantasy with your faithful tributing servants. Your tributing submissives should be referred to as your subs (or your slaves, service pigs, worthless flesh, and so on.)

First contact

Whether on phone or via email, your first conversation is an important opportunity to establish rapport. Your client should trust your skills and experience *even* if they are looking to be completely brutalized or degraded. Remember, your client generally wants the *fantasy version* of the beat down, interrogation, or judicial punishment and they will generally tell you in the negotiation if they like to have their limits pushed. Allow them to talk freely, but for legal and personal privacy concerns, you will need to be guarded with what you say in response. It is generally a good idea to have a few prepared lines to answer difficult questions, and don't disclose too much about your sessions over the phone. You may ask clients to fill out a brief questionnaire that covers experience, interests, specific fantasies, and important medical concerns and restrictions before even having a phone conversation. Many ladies will *only* allow clients to contact them initially via email due to safety and personal reasons, however, you will find that once you become skilled at leading a structured conversation, you will get more sessions if you allow your prospective bottoms to contact you by phone.

Structured conversation - As a kinky professional who is selling her personality, looks, charms, and skills, you will want to qualify the person calling you for a session, find out if their interests are compatible with your own, and finally, book the session. The first contact should be brief, and you should *not* allow your callers to ramble on and on. Remember, you are your own boss and your time is valuable. Once you qualify the person based on interests and have addressed any safety and medical concerns, quickly find out when they will want to see you.

Quality Time, Quality People - A good salesperson will quickly find out how serious a person is about buying their product or service before they waste their time on a sales pitch. Similarly, you need to quickly ascertain when the caller wants to see you before you waste ten to even 20 minutes on the phone with them. You can do this in a very diplomatic fashion unless it is your style to be the Queen Bitch, however, I have found that you can catch more flies with honey, while still maintaining your air of unattainability.

There are three types of callers who will contact you.

The motivated sub - has financial resources to see you and is motivated to make an appointment after he chats with you awhile to determine compatibility. The motivated sub is generally polite and usually experienced with the protocol and expectations of a Mistress from past experience.

The nasty talker - will call you and immediately starts making dirty conversation on the phone. You may get a session with nasty talker, but don't allow him to lead the conversation. As long as he doesn't cross the line with his language, and as long as he understands the parameters of your terms and your services, get him to set an appointment, and don't continue the conversation if he will not commit to a time.

The time sucker - may genuinely want to see you, but either does not have the financial resources, or is nervous about coming to see you. Time sucker is not usually a prankster, and although it is true that on occasion you will get a session from time sucker, generally he will call you at inconvenient times and bore you with his endless prattle. Time sucker calls repeatedly, asks the same questions again and again, and will go into ornate detail about his fantasies, but never commits to an appointment time.

It is my own practice to lead the conversation, meaning to ask very clear and concise questions that the caller must answer. Here is an example

Mistress Q - Hello **submissive mike** - Hello, I'm calling about your ad online. I saw your photo with the amazing thigh high boots with lots of hardware.

Mistress Q- Yes, I know the one! Tell me about your fetishes.
submissive mike- I am a slave, body and soul, to a Goddess with beautiful, sweaty feet. I am interested in boot worship, mild degradation, and face sitting.

Mistress Q - I would love to have you worship my boots! I don't disclose all the details of my session over the phone, but why don't you come by and we can chat in person before we play?
When would you like to come and see me?

submissive mike - I was hoping later today around five pm. Can you tell me a bit about how much your tribute is?

Mistress Q - Yes, my tribute is 150 for half an hour, and 250 for one hour. Come to the corner of Broadway and 32nd and call me from there for exact directions at ten to five.

submissive mike - Perfect - and also, will you do collar and leash training?

Mistress Q - Yes, I will discuss more about my sessions at the in person meeting.

submissve mike - Wonderful! I'll see you at five pm.

Here is an example in which Mistress Q led the conversation, asking a direct, open ended question about sub mike's fantasies which did not require her to disclose too much on her own end about her sessions. Remember, BDSM is a legal "gray area" and you don't know whether you are about to be pranked or recorded, so for your own safety, it's better to say as little as possible on the phone. The Mistress made it clear that she would like to see sub mike, and determined his level of commitment immediately by asking him to make an appointment. If mike began to waffle at that point, unless he was asking more details about the session, the best approach for the Mistress would have been for her to ask sub mike to call back the day that he wanted the session.

Although often, regular subs will be very good about keeping appointments, I generally don't take more than 24 hours advance appointments from a new client UNLESS I have had an in person meeting with them and can judge their level of seriousness and commitment. Although you may be better trained, more educated, and practice with more integrity than your local attorney, the fact of the matter is that sex workers are not considered by most people to be professional in the same way that dentists, mechanics, and aestheticians are, and you will find that you have a fair amount of flakers, especially in the beginning. It is also important to realize that many of your clients will be calling spontaneously when they find they suddenly have some free time to themselves, or when they are in an especially sexy mood. When the mood has passed or their time is occupied with something else, they will no longer be interested in seeing you.

The following is an example in which you should disengage -

Mistress Q- Hello **nasty pig tony** - Hi sweetie, I saw your ads online. I'm looking to do full body worship. I want to lick you all over.

Mistress Q- I want to be very clear that I am a Dominatrix, and I do *NOT* provide sex or escort services. I also require that my submissive address me as "Mistress" or "M'am."

nasty pig tony - Sorry Mistress. Oh, but baby, your photos look so hot in that tight latex dress.
So no GFE?

Mistress Q - No, however, if you feel that you need a punishment for your nasty behavior and disrespect towards women, I can provide you with the correction that you deserve.

nasty pig tony - Yes, but I want to stick my tongue in your ass hole!
Mistress Q - (hang up)

You can't win with this caller, and most likely, he's probably masturbating while talking to you. Just hang up and don't waste your time. Also be aware of the time sucker who will call multiple times in one week and ask you about your schedule, tribute, and more again and again but never get a session. Screening calls and emails are 50% of what you will do with your time, and if you do it well it will result in lots of compatible contacts and sessions.

Requests for Services You Don't Provide

You will often get calls from those individuals who want services that are illegal, or that you don't provide or feel comfortable with. Most of the time, one or two activities not provided will not be a deal breaker for the client, and you will get more sessions if you allow them to come and meet with you without discussing the details, however, sometimes clients will call with specific requests, such as nude face sitting, full body or yoni worship, or roman or brown showers. If they are very insistent upon getting you to admit that you provide one particular service, they might be either a law enforcement official who calls everyone on the list to see who will incriminate herself on the phone, or a very inexperienced person who does not understand appointment booking protocol. Even if you make it clear that your tribute is accepted for your time, and your time only, some bottoms will become upset if you do not provide a specific service that was requested in the initial consultation. Your best bet is to be completely honest and tell them that you do not provide these services. This will allow you to avoid any sticky situations when they arrive, and any arguments after the fact regarding tributes and expectations.

Set the Appointment!

It's up to you to decide how many times to chat with someone who might be a little nervous, but ultimately, the goal of the conversation is to get your caller to make an appointment. Keep your phone and email contact brief and don't give out too much information unless it is about your level of training, experience, and or safety issues to put the caller's mind at ease. If you maintain a good website with a full bio, history, photos, and film clips, you can tell your caller to visit your website for more information, which minimizes the time that you will need to spend on the phone. In fact, smart Dominas make it a requirement to read through their website before they allow submissives to contact them.

Business Phones and Storing Numbers

It is best that you have a separate phone or a call forwarding number for your BDSM calls, not only so that you can protect your privacy and shield your personal times when you are with vanilla friends and family, but also so that you can store regular callers, almost all of whom will be named "mike," "john,"and "steve,"in your contact list. You will not only want to store your good clients names but also the harassers and time suckers who you don't want to talk to. It is nice to give them little nicknames so that you can jog your memory when they call. For instance, I have "sissy-boy-john/jean," "Greek-boot-lover," and "heavy-cor-pun," in my phone, as well as "Russian-time waster," and "knife-freak," who get ignored when they call.

Meeting in Person

On occasion, with a new client who wants a very long involved session, or with a person who you get a funny vibe from on the phone, you may want to meet at a public place which is well lit and where other people are present. If I feel that a caller is shifty on the phone, or if they seem obsessive, sometimes I ask them to meet me at a local coffee house for ten to fifteen minutes so that I can check them out before I invite them back to my home. When you meet at a public place, you can back out or turn away the caller more easily than if they are already at your home or dungeon space. I personally have never been physically attacked by a sub contacting me from an ad, however, it is always a possibility and something that you should take precautions to protect yourself from. This is one of the reasons that I strip bottoms naked and put them in cuffs immediately upon arrival, so that I already have the upper hand. (The very submissive bottoms really love this, anyway.)

For callers who ask for very involved sessions, I generally ask to have them meet me at a public place which is convenient for me, but not necessarily a place that I spend a lot of time at, reducing the possibility that they might "accidentally run into me" on purpose at some time in the future. The place should also be quiet enough to allow for a reasonable conversation. Neither you or your sub want to end up screaming over the table about forced feminization, orgasm denial, or puppy training so that the whole place can hear about it. Show up well dressed, but be conservative enough so that you will not attract too much undue attention. Most of my bottoms are serious professionals who want to be reasonably discreet.

Email, Signatures and Disclaimers
Needless to say, with the preponderance of free webmail available online, there is absolutely no reason that you should not maintain a dedicated email account which is only used for your Dominatrix work. Your email address should be reasonably easy to remember and spell, since you will be spelling it quite a lot over the phone to various people, including the account representatives for your advertising.

It is good business practice to create a signature with a link to your website, as well as your phone number so that your contacts can easily find you. In addition, you may want to put a "disclaimer" in your signature, as is a common practice of many Dommes, or have an automated reply set up on your account.

Your disclaimer is brief, and is generally used for legal reasons. Here is an example of a good one.

> *Mistress Q is a BDSM professional, and receives tribute for time only. No illegal services are provided, and all activities occur between mutually consenting adults.*

Here is an example of an automated response email:

Hello,

Mistress Q has received your email, and will be contacting you within the next 24 hours.

Please be advised that if you want to contact me more quickly, you can reach me at my phone number, 333 - 444- 5555.

In the meantime, I have lots of information about me on my website http://MistressQFetishDiva.com

Regards,
Mistress Q

Referrals

Referrals are another way to verify that your prospective submissive is generally interested. It is becoming more and more common practice for subs to give you another Dominant's email who will "vet" for him. The best way to check out a bottom you have some misgivings about is to get feedback about him from another professional who will likely be very honest about both the good and less favorable qualities in him. Referrals are especially used when Dominas have reason for suspicion when a new sub contacts them. They may feel that the sub might be expecting services that she does not provide, or perhaps she may have personality or personal safety concerns regarding meeting with the bottom in question.

A request for a referral should be brief. Identify yourself and provide a link to your website or other online presence, and let the other Domina know that a specific sub has contacted you for a certain type of session. Remember to provide his email and phone number, because if the Lady providing the referral is like most Pro-Dommes, she will have had contact with several hundred people in one week. Also, request that she tell you a little about the sub's personality, whether he was respectful, and whether she would recommend playing with him. Here is an example

Hello Lady Wednesday,

I was recently contacted by sub john from Hoboken. He let me know that he had seen you for some time and I was wondering if you could tell me a bit about him, his interests, and why you stopped seeing him.

His email is cuck_oo987@hostmail.com and his number is 123-456-7899

Thanks for your feedback!

Arrivals

After booking an appointment, it is common practice to give your bottom an intersection or location near your home or dungeon to call from, rather than immediately giving out your address. There are several reasons for this, mostly having to do with safety concerns. When you have your client call from a nearby location before giving out your home or dungeon address, you can be sure exactly who will be showing up because they will have called you five to ten minutes prior to arriving. You will not have to worry about pranksters who call to get your address and then do not show up for a session. It also prevents clients from showing up too early for sessions and running into other bottoms leaving your place. If sub p has an appointment at 3pm, but he arrives early at 2:30, he will not have the address and will not run into prestigious lawyer slave m, who wants to remain discreet and is still in session with you at 2:30 when sup p arrives. Having your client call also affords you a few more minutes to light candles, adjust the music, lace your thigh high boots, or finish any other small tasks necessary before you begin your next session.

I always ask all my clients, including repeat clients who already have my address, to call me five to ten minutes before arriving so that I can be ready, not only physically, but psychologically as well, when they arrive.

Time Management

As a Pro-Domme, you work for yourself, and as such, you will be managing your own time. You will have to figure out how to balance your time available for sessions as well as your personal time, determine what hours to work, and when to take breaks and holidays.

Depending upon where you live and what the demographics are like in your city, you may work different types of hours. When I lived in LA, I found that the majority of my well paid sessions with regular clients came on weekends and at night, after business hours and rush hour traffic. In NYC, however, what I discovered was that 90% of my sessions came during the hours of 11am to 5pm, and that I rarely got requests after 9pm in the evening. Weekends were usually slow, except during the summer. The reason for this, I found out from other Dommes at the dungeon that I worked at, was that there are quite a few businessmen who commute into the city from other areas like New Jersey and Long Island, who had to fit in "business lunches" with you before they went back to their families in the evening. In Cleveland Ohio, I seemed to be getting requests at all times of day, even as early as nine and ten in the morning! This was rather counter-intuitive, but I have personally found that my absolute best days tend to be Tuesdays, Wednesdays, and Thursdays. The middle of the weeks seems to be the time when most people can get away from family and pressing business needs.

The good news is that most holidays, your usual callers will be with their friends and family, which means that you will be able to "go with the flow" and have Christmas, Thanksgiving, and Super Bowl events without risking the loss of too many session requests. Huge sports events days tend to be slow, however, that doesn't mean you might not get a sudden request from someone who doesn't give a damn about NBA finals on occasion.

Your Schedule

If you are a student or work a second job, keeping a regular availability schedule is even more important so that your regulars can set appointments with you. In your ads and on your website, make it clear that you are available on Tuesdays, Wednesdays, and Thursdays, for instance, and that you are not around Mondays and Fridays. You may want to make yourself available for longer hours when you first start out so that you can determine the "sweet spot" when you get a lot of requests, however, the truth is that when you are a Dominatrix, you will oftentimes need to take sessions here and there at times that are beyond your usual availability window. You will need to possess a certain spontaneity of spirit, because the impulse to see a Dominatrix is something that often comes for the less submissive callers when they feel most turned on, and when that impulse passes they will not call again until it returns.

Your makeup and hair should be done before the times that you are available, that way you can simply refresh your powder and lipstick and get dressed to be ready to go. If you work from a home play space, make sure that it is clean, organized, and ready to take sessions so that when you turn on your phone you are effectively immediately open for business. Don't do errands or other personal things unless you can be home within ten minutes of a call. If you rent dungeon space by the hour, you will need to put your equipment and clothing in your car or travel bag and will need to be waiting at a location within 30 minutes to one hour of your dungeon space. Most of your first time callers will not make appointments in advance! They will be calling you when the impulse strikes them and if you are not ready in a reasonably amount of time, they will simply call the next Lady who is!

Posting Ads
You will need to post most of your ads on sites like Pandemos, OpenAdultDirectory, and ErosGuide much in advance of the time that you want to work, however, for some sites like Backpage and CityVibe, you will want to post or repost your ad at the time that you are immediately available, that way, your ad will be close to the top, and you will have maximum visibility. Once you have determined what your best times are for maximum productivity (calls and sessions) you will want to post your ads as close to those times as possible, and if you can, repost your ads once or twice so that you will have the best possible visibility. Remember that the amount of response that you get will be directly in proportion to the amount and quality of your advertising. Post good quality photos and spend time writing good ad copy that you can simply cut and paste into your ad when you are ready. Always link your website, blog, or other online presence to your ads so that prospective callers can find out more about you, minimizing the time that you will have to spend talking about your life experience via phone and email.

Checking Email and Returning Calls
Remember, at least half of your time will be spent screening emails and calls. I have found that what works for me is to check my email around ten am. By that time I will already have 20 or more emails that have been sent to me overnight. Checking and returning email and calls early is the best way to get the momentum rolling for later in the day. You will need to keep checking and returning mail throughout the day in between sessions. Your ability to get sessions is directly related to your ability to

screen your calls and emails effectively, as well as your conversation skills and your ability to get your callers to set appointments.

Late Night Sessions

Serious callers contact me between 11am and 10:30-11pm. Very late night callers who call later than that tend to be drunk or under the influence of some other illicit substance, and usually call everyone on the list hoping to get someone who will pick up the phone. They often tend to be incoherent, slur their words, and most likely are too inebriated to make their way over to you, even if they genuinely *do* want to see you. For this reason I turn off my phone around 11pm, and I accept late night sessions only by appointment earlier in the day. Those who call the same day who want to see you at a later time will usually show up reasonably on time and be well behaved and fully coherent.

Seasonal Slowdowns

Even the best of the best Divas will experience lulls in demand for their precious time. When you are busy can be a function of your location and demographics in your area. Thanksgiving, and Christmas season, as well as tax season tends to be slow. You should always be prepared and ready to go, *especially* on slow days when you may get an immediate request, but it is okay to work on side projects and do small personal errands that can be easily put aside when you get your call. During slow times the frequency and type of advertising that you do is especially important. Keep posting and reposting at "sweet spot" times. Save money and pay down credit cards when you are busy, so that you will be able to handle slow downs. During your busy times, you can expect three to even four sessions a day, while on slow days you may not have any at all.

Personal Time

Your personal time is just that, personal time! Don't answer calls, and check email only periodically during your personal time. It is hard enough for most vanilla types to know that their friend, girlfriend, or wife is working as a Dominatrix without having to listen to them screen their calls or talk about their sessions in front of them. You may want to set up auto-reply messages for your email and texts so that your callers know that you will be getting back to them soon, but are unavailable at that particular moment. Finding the right balance between work and personal time is one of the hardest things to learn for those who are self-employed, but it is the most important for your quality of life.

Tribute

What is Tribute?
Tribute is considered to be money or gifts given to Dominatrices for the privilege of their time and company. Tribute is given for time, and the amount asked for depends upon your talent, demand for your services, and the location that you live in. In more affluent communities, you will likely be able to command a larger tribute that you would in a more rural area. If you are getting four or more sessions a day, you should likely be able to get higher tributes. The average tribute asked by Pro-Dominas can be anywhere between 200-300 for one hour, but very well known Dominas are known to command more.

For legal reasons, your tribute is accepted for your time, and your time *only.* To protect yourself, don't adjust your tribute to the type of session, however, once you gain experience with the telephone screening process, it is okay to ask for different tributes from different clients depending upon their ability to pay and your enjoyment of the session.

How Much to Ask?
How much you will ultimately ask for your tributes depends upon many factors, including demand for your time, the rate that other Pro-Dommes in your area are asking, the types of equipment that you have, and the ability of your subs to pay your asking rate. When you first start out, it is a better idea to ask for a lower tribute while you gain experience and build up your equipment arsenal. New Ladies always get lots of calls from subs who make the rounds to all the Pros in your area. The first few months that you start out are very important times to establish yourself, your skills, and build relationships with clients who will see you again and again.

Outcalls vs Incalls - Most Pros ask higher tributes for outcalls, because of the travel time, tolls, gas expense and packing and unpacking necessary to take the session. It is okay to ask a sub who lives a considerable time away to give you a small advanced payment such as 50.00 by PayPal, Bitcoin, or other means to cover your gas and travel expenses before you arrive. I only do this when considering a session that would be more than a 45 minute drive away, because it will scare away some prospective submissives who need to be very discreet, but for longer trips, asking for a small upfront tribute is a good way to gauge how serious your prospective sub is about doing the session and avoid the waste of time and aggravation that might result from a long drive to a sub who ends up being a flaker. Often, if they are not willing to commit to a small payment up front, they will not be serious about doing the full session once you arrive.

Types of Payments
Of course, all Dominants love and accept cash, and some Dominants will *only* accept cash, but it is possible to accept other types of tribute without needing to get a business license or a DBA account.

PayPal - PayPal accounts are free, and allow peer to peer users to send "gifts" of cash. Make sure that your tribute is sent as a "gift" unless you have a business license and are filing taxes for your income. PayPal is almost as instant as cash, and you will receive an email within one minute of payment notifying you of your funds.

Bitcoin - Bitcoin is a great way to accept tribute for several reasons. It is reasonably anonymous, which clients like, and payments can be sent that will not show up on their credit card statements for their wives and other family members to look through. Bitcoin is quick and easy and can be sent using any smart device, and it is also accepted by Backpage, which is one of the top sites for ProDomme advertising.

Gift Cards - I do on occasion accept gift cards from clients that I trust, but there are certain pitfalls to accepting gift cards. The main problem with gift cards is that you will have to use the card at the specific retailer that the card is from, unless you decide to trade for Bitcoin on Paxful, for which you will always pay a premium, often upwards of 20% of the value that you will be getting in Bitcoin. Visa and Mastercard gift cards are the only kind of gift cards that I will consider, other than Amazon.

Clips4Sale - The majority of Pro-Dommes who create a career out of their passion for BDSM have a Clips4Sale account online. Your Clips account will not only allow you to have passive income every month from subs who download and pay for your clips, but it also allows you to place a tribute button on your account homepage so that submissive men can tribute you just to show their appreciation. Clips4Sale does take a percentage from your Clips sold and your tributes, so I don't generally accept these types of tributes for sessions. It is nice to have, however, and a good way to put up video that might be banned from YouTube that you can use for self promotion.

Wishlist - If you maintain a wishlist on stockroom.com, amazon.com or another website, on occasion your submissive may ask to send you an outfit that you might wear for him, or a toy that you would like to play with together as part of or all of your tribute. This type of scenario is one of the few occasions that you will need to make sure your tribute is given in advance of the session, and your negotiation as far as what you will accept should be very clear and agreed upon in writing (email or text) so that you will be able to reference your conversation in the event of a She said - he said scenario.

When to Adjust Your Tribute

There are times when you will decide to accept less tribute than you would normally ask. You may have a very sincere sub who wants to see you, is polite and appreciative of you, but who simply cannot afford to pay your rate. You may be experiencing a holiday lull right before Thanksgiving or tax time and have elected to accept less tribute. There are very, very few times when you should reduce your tribute, and don't make a habit out of letting your subs beg and plead for your time at a reduced rate. Your time is valuable, and you may be missing out on other sessions with subs who will pay your rate when you accept the sub who will give the reduced tribute. Most of the time when you accept a reduced tribute it should be for a sub who you really enjoy playing with, who is loyal and faithful, or who you have been in conversations and who intrigues you. Don't reduce your tribute when you feel that playing with a certain person or taking a certain type of session would not make you happy, and don't do it when you feel that you are not being compensated appropriately for your time.

When adjusting your tribute, also consider your expenses that you incur during the course of your work such as equipment, cleaning supplies, gloves, and twine, and advertising costs, as well as the value of your time. In the first few months that you work, you should determine the rate that you are comfortable with, and be very firm with you callers about your rate. In the case of a holiday lull, step up your advertising efforts before considering any reduction in tribute asked. Quite often, just 20 to

50 dollars worth of advertising will bring in several hundred worth in sessions.

Taxes

Believe it or not, is is possible to file taxes and claim your cash income (and your deduction entitlements) when you work as a Pro-Domme. While many Dommes do not do this unless they own a professional dungeon, this information is useful to know because for many Ladies, their Pro-Domme work is their sole or major stream of income. It can be virtually impossible to obtain credit, finance a car, or find an apartment without proof of income, but just one year of taxes and three months of bank statements are often sufficient to obtain lines of credit.

As a Pro-Domme, you can file as an entertainer (look for the tax code under artists and creative industries) and would need to file a schedule C for a self employed individual to claim your deductions. Keep records and receipts of all your expenses, including advertising, business cards, marketing and self promotion expenses such as photography, and clothing used specifically for your Dominatrix work. You can also deduct business travel expenses and pretty much any equipment and supplies that you buy for exclusive use for your work. Be aware that if you are audited, you will have to furnish records and be able to justify how you use your equipment for your work. It should be easy to write off floggers, dungeon furniture, cameras used to make videos, your cellular phone expenses, and even specific kinds of highly theatrical makeup used only for your sessions. Consult with a kink friendly accountant from one of your leather groups for more information about filing taxes and approved deductions.

Traveling Tips

Traveling can be a good way to meet new prospective clients, and it is sometimes necessary to take sessions when you are on the road to conventions, kinky events, or on the way to a personal engagement. Here are a few tips for working on the road.

Choosing a Hotel

Choose your hotel mainly for proximity to the location that you want to work in, as well as other factors, like the client's ability to enter and exit the room discreetly. I personally prefer hotels which do not require clients to enter into a main lobby, firstly for client privacy, but also because there is generally less of a concern for noise when there is not a main hallway that everyone passes through. It is best to try to stay at the same hotel chain when traveling and staying at multiple hotels, because the rooms in the same hotel chain will have very similar furnishings, and you will be able to set up the room in exactly the same way each time. This is important for your own comfort and head space, and it will also minimize confusion about where to find equipment, and reduce likelihood of forgetting items when you pack up to leave. Avoid hotels that are too "ritzy" or expensive for reasons of privacy and discretion, but also because in nice hotels, other guests will complain about noise. Also, you don't want to be responsible for expensive damages at a very nice place.

Packing Equipment

You will need a very sturdy suitcase with wheels, or a large sized tool storage trunk with wheels for traveling. Before selecting your suitcase, make sure that it will fit in the trunk of your car, and consider how easy it might be to lift it up and down a flight or two of stairs, and consider how you might be able to pack your equipment inside.

Obviously, you will need to scale down with respect to the diversity and size of the equipment that you bring. I have short riding crops, smaller wooden paddles for travel use, and I pack things like shoelaces, twine and smaller CBT devices in different colored travel pouches and cosmetic organizers so that I can quickly identify where my equipment is and easily pack and unpack items. Netting bags used for washing delicate laundry items are good for packing small items of clothing in, and I use good quality, sturdy plastic storage containers for delicate items like wooden clothespins and clover clamps, and have even fashioned my own travel aluminum tin (lined with foam) for the glass components of my violet wand. By repacking my items, they take up much less space in the suitcase, and will reduce the number of suitcases that I will have to bring with me. Pack heavier items like metal cuffs, shackles and weights for CBT near the bottom of the suitcase, so that it will not be top heavy and unwieldy.

Pack for easy accessibility! It is not unusual that you might make a house call or two in between stops at different cities that you visit, and you will want to be able to quickly take out the equipment you want to use without having to completely unpack your entire suitcase. This is another reason why plastic storage containers, organizers, and bags are very important.

When deciding whether or not to pack an item, consider how often you get requests for that item, and how useful it would be on the rare occasion that you do get a request for it. You may want to pack your essentials in one suitcase, and equipment used less often in another tote or canvas bag which you can leave in your car and bring out only if it is requested.

Other Items to Pack When Traveling

Extension cords - Not all hotels will have outlets in convenient places. Bring a minimum of a ten foot extension cord to a maximum of 20. Anything longer will be too bulky and unnecessary, and shorter cords may not cover the distance that you need.

Dirty Bags - to separate dirty cross dressing lingerie, used shoelaces for CBT, other equipment that you might need to clean in a specific way.

Charging Devices - for laptops, tablets, smart devices, and equipment.

One extra towel - The extra towel is for yourself, and should be a color other than white. You will be assured that you will always have a clean towel even if you have four clients in one day and they all take showers.

Travel Sized Cleaners - Pre-packaged leather wipes, disinfecting wipes for non-wood, non-leather items, and flat spray bottles of alcohol found in the medical section at drugstores. You may want to put anything that has the potential to leak in a zip lock bag, to prevent accidental damage to other items in your suitcase in the event of an accident.

Travel Sized Toiletries - You will be packing a lot of heavy equipment for your work, so it is a good idea to minimize the size, bulk, and weight of everything else that you pack. Travel toiletries are one of the best ways to conserve space in your suitcase, and can be found easily at any drugstore or cosmetics outlet.

A Wrap Dress, or Long Lightweight Jacket - There will be times when you need to go to the front desk, to the vending machine, laundry, or out to your car, and will not want to completely undress in order to do that. Having a wrap style dress that can be thrown on over your clothing, or a knee length jacket is a quick and easy way to be able to step out without having to unlace your corset or peel off your latex suit.

Non-perishable food - It's a good idea to have instant noodles, canned chili, uncut fruit, and other non-perishable food with you. You may become so busy that you do not have time to eat, and not all locations will have restaurants that deliver. If your hotel have a fridge or if you take a cooler you might be able to pack other items that need cold storage, that way you will not have to dress/undress, and redo your makeup when you have to step out, which takes time away from productivity and availability. I know that I have had quite a few instances in which I get last minute calls for sessions late in the evening which prevented me from being able to get food before bed. Most hotels provide tea/coffee and hot water in the lobby, and may in addition have a small kitchenette with fridge and microwave in the room or another public place in the hotel.

Small sized speaker - for music, a very important part of your mood, and also a good way to conceal some of the noise from the session.

Scarves, colored light bulbs, or LED or wax candles - an important part of creating the mood. Use scarves to drape over lamp shades to create a more low light effect, or replace light bulbs with party bulbs, but don't forget to remove them!

Ads

Put out "teaser ads" one to two weeks before visiting a certain city to see how many requests you get for your services. Sites like Eros and Pandemos allow you to post visiting ads, but will not yield good results unless you post at least two weeks in advance. A good rule of thumb is that for every 20 emails or calls you get, four to five of those will actually see you in person. Remember to confirm with clients from other cities a day or two before you arrive, but keep in mind that even with confirmation, you will get a fair amount of flakers. Always post on instant visibility advertising sites like Backpage and Cityvibe the same day that you arrive, in addition to a week or two before.

Out of State Contacts- and Listserve

Give special labels to out of state contacts. You may want to put the state or city identifiers before their name, as in CT-john-sub, or Philly-michael-heavyCP. Make sure to get permission from your clients before putting them on a listserve, since many of them may have family members or partners who also access their emails, but it is a good idea to put as many subs as possible on your listserve for a certain region. Sending a group listserve is another good way to notify clients that you will be coming, and is much less expensive than advertising.

Shopping Resources on the Road

Drugstores and Dollar Stores
Alcohol
Baby wipes
Batteries for equipment

Candles
Chocolate sauce, honey
Chopsticks (for CBT)
Cleaners
Clothespins
Condoms
Cosmetic pouches
Cotton balls
Duct tape
EMT scissors
Exam gloves
Extension cords
Feather dusters (sensation play)
First aid supplies
Lighters
Muscle rub (for CBT)
Rubber Bands (CBT aid)
Sleep masks (blindfolds)
Paper towels
Party bulbs
Pet collars and leashes
Saran wrap (mummification)
Sharps containers
Sleep masks (blindfolds)
Stockings/nylons
Storage bins and tins
Tens units (only some locations)
Toothpase (for CBT)
Twine

Wooden Spoons and spatulas

**Hardware
Stores-**
Bamboo
gardening
stakes
(canes)
Biners, carabiners
Chain
Extension cords
Metal O-rings (CBT)
Paint sticks (spanking)
Rope
Tool Boxes and storage
Twine
Wooden dowels and screw eyes (spreader bars)
Vises

Military Surplus Stores
Bandanas (blindfolds/gags)
Boot Laces (CBT)
Canvas cags and cases for equipment
Earplugs
First aid kits
Gas masks
Goggles
Handcuffs (sometimes, if they also sell novelty)
Knives
Lighters

Military clothing
Paracord
Rope
Ski masks (hoods)
Snake bite kits (NP)

Sporting Goods
Boxing Gloves
Fishing weights (CBT)
Snake bite kits (NP)
Work out apparel

Thrift Stores
Inexpensive large sized lingerie (x-dressing)
Inexpensive large sized clothing (x-dressing)
Various Clothing Items

Adult Specialty Stores (larger cities)
Fetish specific clothing
BDSM supplies

Personal Slaves

As a Pro-Domina, you will be inundated with requests from men who want to do your bidding and satisfy your needs. It will be necessary to determine which requests are genuine, and who you should decline. Generally, you will need to consider how much time you have and how many personal slaves you would feel comfortable taking on simultaneously. Remember that having a personal slave is a relationship, even if you do not engage in sexual intercourse. These relationships may last for many years and are generally as intimate as close friendships and romantic partnerships. I have heard of Dominant Ladies having several personal slaves at one time, but it is rare that someone might have more than three unless a few of them are casual, non-committal relationships.

BDSM/Fetish and Personal Compatibility

It should go without saying that you should enjoy the same sorts of play. Even if your sub simply wants to offer domestic service, it is should be understood that your sub will be sharing a considerable amount of time with you. Some Dommes choose subs or slaves who have particular types of skills to offer that are useful to them, such as web design, photography, or carpentry skills, In general though, you should choose your relationships mainly with the interests of personal compatibility and mutually enjoyed activities if you want to have long term, happy relationships.

Loyalty Tests

Before taking on a personal sub or slave, allow them to serve you on several occasions to determine their level of reliability and loyalty, and also to determine how much you enjoy playing with them. Does their schedule align with your own? Do they want to be full time or part time? How open are they about their submissiveness or slavery? Be careful not to take on a slave who is self serving, and who simply wants to get good times from you without giving back to his Mistress. I get three or more requests each week from men who want to be "personals," however, upon further investigation, asking their schedule and availability and finding out that they don't have time, I determine fairly quickly that they are just trying to get free sessions and are not genuine in their attempts to be personal, long term, dedicated slaves.

Ordeals
As an initiation rite, you may want to put your submissive through one or more ordeals before they might be allowed to serve you as a personal slave. The type of ordeal that you choose depends upon your preferences. An ordeal is a test of your sub's willpower, strength of character, and commitment to you in that they must complete the task in order to show their dedication to you.

Collaring a sub/slave
A sub or slave who has shown faithful and loyal service and who makes his Mistress very happy can be given a collar in recognition of his dedication to his Mistress. Often, collaring a slave is a ceremony that takes place with kinky friends and leather family and has just as important significance as a marriage vow. Giving a sub/slave a collar is a way to acknowledge their service and let them know that you are happy with them, and will be accepting their service for a long time. There are other good books which discuss BDSM in the context of personal relationships which can address this topic in greater depth. Dominance and submission in the context of a relationship will involve issues which are much more complex and does not fall within the scope of this book.

BDSM Terminology

This Glossary covers terms used in the book which may not have been discussed in detail, as well as common terms and abbreviations which you may run across online that are useful to know. These are general terms which may be nonspecific to Pro-Domme work, and there are terms for illegal acts which have been included for informational purposes.

Aftercare - first aid and emotional support that a Dominant provides to the bottom after a session.

B & D - Bondage and Domination

Bastinado - a style of punishment used in very conservative cultures as in ancient Persia. Canes or sometimes heavier wooden pieces are used to strike the bottom of the feet.

BDSM - Bondage, Domination, Sado-masochism

Biner - a metal devices which is used to secure BDSM equipment to another object. Found at any hardware store.

Bondage Bed - a padded table with hardware that allows for a sub to be quickly bound and immobilized. Bondage beds often have cages built into them, or other special features that facilitate BDSM play.

Bottom - the person who is on the receiving end of BDSM. Bottoms may or may not be submissive or masochistic. A bottom is a generic term for the person who is under control of the Dominant.

Branding - an insignia (sign of ownership) which is burnt into a bottom's skin.

Brown Showers - Poop play

Burn Speed - the amount of movement necessary to create a burning sensation and mild abrasions on a rope bottoms skin. Hemp rope has a low burn speed, meaning that it is easier to create abrasions, while cotton rope has the highest burn speed.

CBT - Cock and Ball Torture. Sado-masochistic actions that punish the male genitals, penis, and scrotum.

CorPun / CP - Corporal Punishment. Refers to any sort of physical punishment but usually associated with paddling, caning, lashing, and judicial or domestic style punishment.

CFNM - Clothed Female Naked Male. A common request for D/s play

Chastity Device - any object which is placed over the penis to prevent erections and sexual intercourse. Medical grade silicone devices, metal cock cages, and the "gates of hell" are all considered chastity devices.

Client - a person who pays for a professional service

Cuck - a cuckold. A cuckold is a man who's romantic partner has sex with someone else, often in his presence, and often as a form of size shaming. Cuckoos are birds which lay their eggs in birds of another species nest, leaving the other bird to care for their offspring. This is where there term originates from.

Cuckie - a derogatory term for a man who is cuckolded

Cutting - usually used to refer to scarification, the act of repeatedly cutting a bottom's skin with the intention of creating a permanent mark or decorative design. Cutting can also refer to cutting knife play.

Dispersed impact - an impact which is not concentrated in a small area, but dispersed over a larger areas. In flogging for instance, each small tail hits a slightly different location on the body, effectively transferring the force to a larger surface area.

Domestic - concerning the home. Domestic punishment refers to punishment that takes place at home, in a domestic setting, and is usually a type of punishment that parents might have used with children at various times in history.

Domme/Domina - A Dominatrix

D/s - Dominance and submission

Fetish - a sexual turn on that comes from an object not usually associated with sex, item of clothing, odor, or non-traditional sexual situation.

FinDom - short hand for financial Domination. FinDom occurs when a Pro-Domme consensually uses a submissive for financial servitude, gifts, and monetary support.

Forced Bi- the act of having a Dominant force a man to be in a sexual situation with another man.

ForcedFem/FF - Forced Feminization or Forced Fem for short
GFE - Girl Friend Experience - a service provided by escorts. Men who also see escorts will sometimes ask for this because they are inexperienced with BDSM.

Greek - Slang term for a man who allows another person to penetrate him anally. This word is banned from most advertising, but you will still be asked about this from subs via email.

GS - Golden Showers. Piss play or the act of a Dominant urinating upon a sub.

Heavy - very intense, as in heavy humiliation, heavy CBT, heavy nipple torture.

Humbler - a locking vice which fits tightly over a man's scrotum, pulling it behind him and preventing him from standing up straight, therefore "humbling" him.

Interrogation - the act of questioning an individual who is usually imprisoned or in captivity. Interrogation is a specialized style of interview which is designed to put the questioned individual under stress in order to extract important information.

Judicial - ordered by law. Judicial punishment is a type of punishment which has been sentenced to an individual for a specific violation of the law. It usually is administered in a public place in front of many witnesses.

Kinkster - a kinky person

Knife Play - usually non-cutting play involving use of a knife. Knife play can be used to arouse the fear response.

Leather Group - a BDSM and fetishists community and social organization

Maestra - the Feminine form of the Italian word for "Master"

Masochist - a lover of pain.

Medical Play - style of play which uses doctor, nurse, or other medical professional and patient role play. Medical equipment is generally used for these sessions.

Milking - usually refers to prostate "milking," the use of fingers or toys in a rocking motion over the prostate. It provides pleasurable sensations and is said to have health benefits for the male.

Mummification - the act of wrapping a submissive in layers of constrictive material, usually saran wrap or shrink wrap.

Novice/Newbie - a person who is new to BDSM play
NP/NT - Nipple Play, which is more sensual, and Nipple Torture, which is more extreme.

Old Guard - Older kinksters who have different protocols and often different behavior expectations and rituals than younger kinksters

Ordeal - a trial specifically designed for an initiate who wants to be accepted into a club or achieve a specific goal. Native American vision quests and college fraternity hazing are ordeals.

Percussive - BDSM play which involves repeated hitting or blows with equipment or body parts

Play Party - A party or gathering where BDSM play or other kinky activities occur

Play Space - a location equipped with BDSM paraphernalia that is used for sessions or scenes.

Pony and Puppy Training - BDSM play that mimics the acts of training these animals.

Predicament Bondage - a situation in which a sub who tries to escape from one position finds himself in an even more uncomfortable position.

Queening - subs who enjoy toilet play using a specially designed chair

Roman Showers - the act of vomiting upon a bottom

S & M - Sadomasochism

Scarification - the same meaning as cutting

Scene - The BDSM and Fetish world and community. This word is sometimes also used to mean a session.

Screw Eye - a piece of hardware that can be screwed into wood or metal which functions as an attachment point for biners, rope, and other bondage equipment. Both screw eyes and biners can be found at any hardware store.

Service Top - A Top who is simply going through the motions in order to please their submissive or bottom.

Session - BDSM playtime

Sharps Container - A bright red medical disposal container used for contaminated sharps, such as hypodermic and acupuncture needles, as well as used scalpel blades.

Shibari - Japanese style bondage used to take prisoners of war. Shibari is considered a martial art.

Silent Alarm - The practice of having a friend call you when you are going to a session to make sure you are safe. Silent alarms are often used by sex workers who do outcalls to a location when they are worried about their safety. An agreed upon word or phrase can be used to alert the caller that something is wrong without having to explain the situation.

Sissy - a man who cross dresses and likes to be trained to be ladylike, demure, and well behaved. Sissy maids and sissy girls like to be dressed in highly feminine, dainty, pretty, clothing.

Size Shaming - the act of humiliating a man with a small penis by criticizing his size, measuring, and it, taking photos, and sometimes posting them on adult sites online.

Sluts - a man who often cross dresses and is highly sexual but takes the submissive role. Sluts dress trampy and like to be made to feel exceptionally dirty.

Spanking horses - a bench which is designed specifically for BDSM punishment, usually padded, and with attachment points for cuffs.

Spreader Bar - a wooden or metal rod with screw eyes at both ends which is attached to cuffs to prevent a submissive prisoner from closing his legs or clasping his hands together.

St Andrew's Cross - a medieval style X shaped wooden cross which prisoners are strapped or bound to so that they can be tortured and interrogated.

Stingy - generally refers to a light pressure sensation which stings. Sensations from a flicker whip, lightweight rubber whip, and bamboo cane are considered stingy. The opposite would be thuddy.

Stockade - a medieval style wooden cage that surrounds the neck and wrists of a prisoner

Strap-on - a phallic object or dildo which is secured to a special harness that is worm over the pelvis. Strap-ons can be used for visual provocation, or for forced oral servitude for the sub, in addition to anal penetration. Strap on worship involves visually appreciating, stroking, and orally appreciating the strap-on worn by a Domina.

Sub - submissive or subservient. Subs desire to please the Dominant in any way possible. Subs may also be masochists but many prefer to avoid pain.

Subspace - an altered state that a bottom enters during BDSM play. A submissive in subspace may have trouble communicating verbally, and is more vulnerable to suggestion. Subspace is caused by hormones such as adrenaline, enkephalins and endorphins as well as the experience of sensory deprivation, emotional highs, and intense sensations.

Switch - a person who sometimes Tops and sometimes bottoms during BDSM play

T&D - Tease and Denial. The act of getting your sub all worked up and then denying him ultimate pleasure. T&D has nothing to do with handjobs, but has to do with the arousal that comes from contact and company from the Domina. Be aware that some clients who ask for T&D are using it as a code for handjobs.

Thuddy - a heavy sensation which causes a dull ache or heavy, lingering pain. Wooden paddles and heavy floggers are thuddy. The opposite is stingy.

Toilet Training - refers to consumption of golden and brown showers

Top Space - an emotional/endorphin high experienced by the Top during BDSM play

Trailer winch- a crank which is used to lift heavy loads. Trailer winches are used for suspension and partial suspension bondage.

TS/TV - Trans-sexual and Transvestite. Transvestites are men who cross dress, while Trans-sexuals are people who are transitioning to another gender, who oftentimes are taking hormones and living life as a different gender than they were born into.

Vanilla - refers to the non-kinky world and conventional sex. Individuals who do not understand or practice BDSM, fetishes, or other kinky practices are considered "vanilla."

Vise - any tool which is used to hold something in place while it is being worked on. In an S/M context, various types of bondage equipment, including humbler devices.

Yoni - the vulva and female genitalia

Worship - the act of a submissive kissing, licking, massaging, or caressing a certain area.
Types of worship include foot, leg, boot, and latex. Latex worship also entails shining the latex. References and Other Reading

Wrapping - Occurs when a whip or cane curves around to the side of the body. Sometimes, this can result in unintended markings and cuts because the momentum increases as the whip wraps around to the front of the body.

References and Recommended Reading

The American Red Cross First Aid Handbook - Published by The American Red Cross Annually.

Screw the Roses, Send Me the Thorns, The Romance and Sexual Sorcery of Sadomasochism, Mystic Rose Books, C 2000 by Phillip Miller and Molly Devon

The Mistress Manual - A Good Girl's Guide to Female Dominance, by Mistress Lorilei, c 2000 by Greenery Press

The Seductive Art of Japanese Bondge, by Midori, c 2001 by Fire Horse Productions, Published by Greenery Press

Sexy Origins of Intimate Things by Charles Panati, c Charles Panati 1998

The Marquis de Sade - 120 Days of Sodom and Other Writings, compiled and translated by Austryn Wainhouse and Richard Seaver, Grove Press, New York

Venus in Furs, by Leopold von Sacher-Masoch, published in 2009 by World Classics books

Jay Wiseman's Erotic Bondage Handbook, c 2000, by Jay Wiseman

About the Author

The Author has been a lifestyle player since her early 20s, and supported herself by working three days per week at a dungeon in Los Angeles while she finished her post graduate degree. During her early 20s, she worked was published several times in fetish related coffee table books and magazines, and appeared in some sex positive, erotic instructional videos for couples. She went on to work in a private healthcare practice for five years on the east coast, while taking fetish/BDSM sessions in her spare time. Over the course of her more than fifteen years as a practicing Dominatrix, she has had the opportunity to learn about all sorts of BDSM practices and play, and it is her wish to convey some of those things to new Dominas as a way to introduce them into the practice of becoming a Dominatrix.

Printed in Great Britain
by Amazon